Revision Notes
for
Standard Grade
Mathematics

Andrew Sinclair

Depute Head Teacher

Mearns Castle High School

Published by
Chemcord
Inch Keith
East Kilbride
Glasgow

ISBN 1 870570 59 6

© Sinclair , 1996
revised edition, 2000
reprint 2005

Printed by Bell and Bain Ltd, Glasgow

About This Book

This book covers all you need to know for Standard Grade Maths at General and Credit Levels. This new revised edition includes the Statistics and non-calculator content added to the syllabus for the 2001 exams.

The first seven chapters cover the seven main topic areas of the syllabus. Chapter 8 gives examples on problem solving. Each chapter is divided into sections to make it easier for you to find a specific topic. All key results are 'boxed' and key terms are shown in **bold like this** so that you can find them quickly.

The main difference between the levels in Standard Grade Maths is the content included in each. All the material in each topic has been grouped together regardless of its level in the syllabus. Consequently, each section has been clearly labelled with the level so that you know exactly which parts you require to study.

The Scottish Qualifications Authority has identified the 'easier' Credit material to allow pupils to attempt Credit Level, without having covered all the topics. Therefore, to make this book useful to as many pupils as possible, the material has been labelled as follows:-

G   All the material required for the **General** Level. If you are trying for General Level and not attempting Credit, this is the work you should concentrate on.

C/G   The **'easier' Credit** Level material. If you are hoping to extend from General Level by trying some Credit Level work you should concentrate on this material, as well as the **G** topics. Check with your teacher if you are not sure if you have covered all these topics - your teacher is the best judge of what is appropriate for you.

C   The **'harder' Credit** Level material. If you are covering the whole Credit course you need to be familiar with all the topics (**G, C/G and C**) in the book.

The **Contents** on pages 2 and 3 gives the general outline of the book. A **Detailed Index** has been added on pages 150 to 154 to help you find particular topics or terms easily.

The book can be used:

as a reference book - when you come across a term or topic that you are unsure about, look up that topic area in the book and refresh your memory, but make sure you understand it properly when you do. Keep the book for reference if you intend to study maths after Standard Grade.

to revise a particular topic - read through the material carefully. Make sure that you know all formulae and standard results. Study the examples given so that you understand how they are worked out. Then try some more examples on the topic from your textbook or jotters.

alongside past papers - in the final lead-up to your exams, the best revision is to work through exam papers from previous years. When you come across a question that you are unable to answer, look up that topic area in the book and see if a similar example is given. With over 200 examples in the book, there is a good chance of finding something that will help.

CONTENTS

Revision Notes for

1. NUMBER

1.1 TYPES OF NUMBERS

C

Most of the work in Standard Grade uses the following sets of numbers:

N   natural numbers   1, 2, 3, 4, 5, ...

W   whole numbers   0, 1, 2, 3, 4, ...

Z   integers   ..., −3, −2, −1, 0, 1, 2, 3, ...

Q   rational numbers   any number that can be written in the form of a fraction,

ie $\dfrac{a}{b}$ where a and b are integers

     irrational numbers   eg $\sqrt{2}$, $\sqrt[3]{5}$, π,   etc

R   real numbers   all rational and irrational numbers

Assume that you are using real numbers unless you are told otherwise.

Sometimes the context of a question will make a restriction on the type of answer, eg non-negative, non-fraction.

1.2 ORDER OF OPERATIONS

G

In any calculation with numbers or algebra, follow the priority order given by the **BODMAS** rule. (Some remember it as **BOMDAS**.)

For operations of equal priority, eg add and subtract, work from left to right.

B rackets
O ff
before
D ivide and
M ultiply
before
A dd and
S ubtract

Example 1:

$3 + (\underline{8 - 3}) \times 2$

$= 3 + \underline{5 \times 2}$

$= 3 + 10$

$= 13$

Example 2:

$5 - \underline{2 \times 6} + 3$

$= \underline{5 - 12} + 3$

$= -7 + 3$

$= -4$

It is safest to write out a new line for each stage in the working and underline what requires to be done next.
Do not rearrange the order of the numbers in the calculation.

Powers like squares, cubes and roots are sometimes called **orders.**

For more complicated calculations, the rule can be remembered with **O** standing for orders.

Remember that each line of a fraction acts as if a bracket is round it.

| **B** rackets off |
| **O** rders |
| before |
| **D** ivide and |
| **M** ultiply |
| before |
| **A** dd and |
| **S** ubtract |

Example 1:

$$3^2 + \frac{4+8}{2}$$

$$= \underline{3^2} + \frac{12}{2}$$

$$= 9 + \frac{12}{2}$$

$$= 9 + 6$$

$$= 15$$

Example 2:

$$4 \times 3^2 - (5-2)^3$$

$$= 4 \times \underline{3^2} - 3^3$$

$$= \underline{4 \times 9} - 27$$

$$= 36 - 27$$

$$= 9$$

1.3 ESTIMATING ANSWERS

Rounding to 1 significant figure (see Section 1.4 for details on rounding) helps with estimating the size of an answer.

Keep in mind the 'golden rule' for calculating:

Estimate ⟶ Calculate ⟶ Check

eg   You should expect the answer to 3452 x 59 ÷ 27 to be approximately 6000, as

3452 x 59 ÷ 27

is approximately equal to

3000 x 60 ÷ 30   (It is easier to do the underlined part first!)

= 3000 x 2

= 6000

Estimating first and checking the answer should help to avoid giving ridiculous answers to questions without noticing!

Use common sense to decide if an answer is likely. You should not expect to pay £20 000 per year to insure a car which costs £12 000.

1.4 ROUNDING

1.4.1 Rounding to Decimal Places (dp) **G**

1. Count the required number of digits after the decimal point, then cut.

2. If the first digit being cut off is:

   5 or more, then round the previous digit up 1,

   less than 5, then leave the previous digit as it is.

   eg $3.6352 = 3.63\underline{5}2 = 3.64$ to 2 dp

   $42.0009 = 42.0\underline{0}09 = 42.0$ to 1 dp

1.4.2 Rounding to Significant Figures (sf) **C/G**

1. Start from the left of the number and ignore any initial zeros.

2. Count from the first non-zero digit and count every digit (including zeros) from there. (Significant figures are shown in bold in the examples.)

3. Round as for decimal places.

   eg $8.2369 = \mathbf{8.236}\underline{9} = 8.24$ to 3 sf

   $0.003\,014 = 0.003\,0\underline{1}4 = 0.003\,0$ to 2 sf

This rule does not help in counting the number of significant figures in a number like 5000, which ends in zeros but has no decimal point showing.

It could have been rounded to:

the nearest thousand,	ie 1 significant figure,
the nearest hundred,	ie 2 significant figures,
the nearest ten,	ie 3 significant figures,
the nearest unit,	ie 4 significant figures.

The context will normally make this clear.

1.4.3 Rounding to an Appropriate Degree of Accuracy

You will often have to decide what accuracy is appropriate based on the context of the question.

For example, depending on the question, a calculator answer of 36.727 272 could correspond to:

37 p	the cost per can of juice	to the nearest penny,
£36.73	an insurance premium	to the nearest penny,
£40	an estimate for a job	to the nearest £10,
36.7°	an angle in a trig calculation	to 1 dp,
37 m	the 3rd side in the triangle shown, given the other two sides	to the same accuracy as the other sides.

For most calculations, 3 significant figures will normally be accurate enough.

You should avoid giving answers with more significant figures than there are in the data given in the question.

1.4.4 Rounding in Practice

Do not round off until the final answer. If a final answer is required correct to 1 dp, and you round off to 1 dp before that, it is unlikely the final answer will end up still correct to 1 dp.

In all the calculations in this book, the first 3 or 4 figures are shown and then '...' to indicate the number continues, eg 3.14... . Only the final answer is rounded.

Example: A square metal plate of side 40 mm has 100 holes of radius 2 mm drilled in it. What area of metal remains (answer correct to 3 sf)?

Area square $= 40 \times 40 = 1600$ mm^2

Area 1 hole $= \pi r^2 = \pi \times 2^2 = 12.5...$ mm^2

Area 100 holes $= 100 \times 12.5... = 1256.6...$ mm^2

Area remaining $= 1600 - 1256.6... = 343.3...$ mm^2 $=$ **343 mm^2** to 3 sf

1.5 NON-CALCULATOR NUMERICAL SKILLS

In the non-calculator paper, you would be expected to be able perform the following operations without the use of a calculator. All are at the **G** level unless indicated.

Whole Numbers: addition and subtraction (up to 4 digits),
multiplication (4 digit by 1 digit / 2 digit by 2 digit),
division (4 digit by 1 digit).

Decimals: addition and subtraction (up to 3 dp),
multiplication and division (3 dp by 1 digit whole number /
3 dp by multiples of 10, 100 or 1000).

Fractions: addition, subtraction and multiplication of simple commonly
used fractions and mixed numbers.
At **C/G** level, addition, subtraction, multiplication and division
of all fractions including mixed numbers.
See Section 1.7.

Percentages: commonly used whole number percentages of numbers.
See Section 1.8.

Integers: addition and subtraction,
multiplication of a 1 digit integer by a 1 digit whole number.
At **C/G** level, multiplication and division.
See Section 1.6.

1.6 INTEGERS (POSITIVE AND NEGATIVE NUMBERS)

1.6.1 Adding and Subtracting Integers

Use a number line to help find the correct answer.

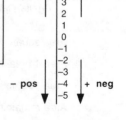

Adding a positive and **subtracting a negative** take you **up** the number line towards the **positive** end.

Adding a negative and **subtracting a positive** take you **down** the number line towards the **negative** end.

eg 　　　$-5 + 3 = -2$ 　　　$-3 + 6 = 3$

　　　　$-5 - 3 = -8$ 　　　$2 - 5 = -3$

Adding a negative is the same as subtracting a positive.

eg $\quad 3 + (-7) = 3 - 7 = -4$

$\quad\quad -2 + (-3) = -2 - 3 = -5$

Subtracting a negative is the same as adding a positive.

eg $\quad 3 - (-5) = 3 + 5 = 8$

$\quad\quad -2 - (-3) = -2 + 3 = 1$

1.6.2 Multiplication of an Integer by a Whole Number

G

At the **G** level, this will only involve multiplication of a single digit negative number by a single digit positive number.

> **A positive times a negative will give a negative.**

eg $\quad 3 \times (-4) = -12$

1.6.3 Multiplication and Division of Integers

C/G

Both multiplication and division follow the same patterns.

pos × **pos** = **pos**
pos × **neg** = **neg**
neg × **pos** = **neg**
neg × **neg** = **pos**

eg $\quad -3 \times 2 = -6$

$\quad\quad -2 \times (-5) = 10$

pos ÷ **pos** = **pos**
pos ÷ **neg** = **neg**
neg ÷ **pos** = **neg**
neg ÷ **neg** = **pos**

eg $\quad -12 \div (-3) = 4$

$\quad\quad \dfrac{18}{-6} = -3$

Number

1.7 FRACTIONS

Fractions are used to represent part of a quantity, or numbers which lie between the whole numbers on the number line.

The term **fractions** usually refers to **common** (or **vulgar**) **fractions**. However decimals and percentages are also types of fractions.

The number on the top line is called the **numerator**. The number on the bottom line is called the **denominator**.

A fraction like $3\frac{4}{5}$ is called a **mixed number**.

When it is written in the form $\frac{19}{5}$, it is called an **improper** or **top-heavy fraction**.

Much of the work on fractions can now be done on a scientific calculator. However the non-calculator paper requires you to work with fractions without using a calculator. The same methods are required for algebraic fractions, so you must know them.

1.7.1 Equivalent Fractions (G)

Fractions which have the same value are called **equivalent fractions.**

You can find an equivalent fraction by multiplying or dividing the numerator and denominator by the same number.

eg $\quad \frac{2}{3}=\frac{2\times5}{3\times5}=\frac{10}{15} \qquad \frac{8}{12}=\frac{8\div2}{12\div2}=\frac{4}{6} \qquad \frac{20}{24}=\frac{20\div4}{24\div4}=\frac{5}{6}$

If it is not possible to divide the numerator and denominator by the same number, you say the fraction is in its **simplest form.**

1.7.2 Adding and Subtracting Fractions (G)

Both addition and subtraction follow similar methods.

1. Find the **lowest common denominator** for the fractions,
   ie the smallest number that both denominators will divide into.

2. Change both fractions to equivalent fractions with that denominator.

10   Revision Notes for

3. Add or subtract the numerators.

4. Simplify if necessary.

Example 1:

$$\frac{3}{5}+\frac{5}{6}$$

$$=\frac{18}{30}+\frac{25}{30}$$

$$=\frac{43}{30}=1\frac{13}{30}$$

Example 2:

$$\frac{2}{3}-\frac{1}{4}$$

$$=\frac{8}{12}-\frac{3}{12}$$

$$=\frac{5}{12}$$

1.7.3 Adding and Subtracting Mixed Numbers

At the **G** level, only commonly used fractions and mixed numbers will be used.

1. Add or subtract the whole numbers first.

2. Add or subtract the fraction parts as for simple fractions.

3. In subtraction, it may be necessary to borrow a whole number and change it into a fraction.

4. Simplify if necessary.

Example 1:

$$5\frac{2}{3}+3\frac{5}{6}$$

$$=8\frac{2}{3}+\frac{5}{6}$$

$$=8\frac{4}{6}+\frac{5}{6}$$

$$=8\frac{9}{6}$$

$$=9\frac{3}{6}$$

$$=9\frac{1}{2}$$

Example 2:

$$3\frac{1}{2}-1\frac{7}{9}$$

$$=2\frac{1}{2}-\frac{7}{9}$$

$$=2\frac{9}{18}-\frac{14}{18}$$

$$=1\frac{27}{18}-\frac{14}{18}$$

$$=1\frac{13}{18}$$

1.7.4 Multiplying Fractions

At the **G** level, only commonly used fractions and mixed numbers will be used.

1. Look for cancelling, ie simplifying by dividing any top number and any bottom number by the same number.

2. Multiply top against top and bottom against bottom.

3. Simplify if necessary.

Example 1:

$$\frac{4}{15} \times \frac{9}{16} = \frac{\cancel{4}^{\,1}}{\cancel{15}_{\,5}} \times \frac{\cancel{9}^{\,3}}{\cancel{16}_{\,4}}$$

$$= \frac{1 \times 3}{5 \times 4}$$

$$= \frac{3}{20}$$

Example 2:

$$\frac{3}{4} \text{ of } 120$$

$$= \frac{3}{\cancel{4}_{\,1}} \times \frac{\cancel{120}^{\,30}}{1}$$

$$= \frac{90}{1} = 90$$

1.7.5 Division of Fractions

The **inverse** of a fraction is obtained by switching the numerator and denominator.

Dividing by a fraction is equivalent to multiplying by the inverse of the fraction.

eg $\div \frac{2}{3}$ is equivalent to $\times \frac{3}{2}$

Example:

$$\frac{3}{15} \div \frac{2}{5} = \frac{3}{\cancel{15}_{\,3}} \times \frac{\cancel{5}^{\,1}}{2}$$

$$= \frac{\cancel{3}^{\,1}}{\cancel{3}_{\,1}} \times \frac{1}{2}$$

$$= \frac{1}{2}$$

1.7.6 Multiplying and Dividing Mixed Numbers

C/G

1. Change all mixed numbers into improper fractions first.

2. Multiply or divide as for simple fractions.

3. Simplify if necessary.

Example 1:

$$3\frac{1}{5} \times 2\frac{1}{4}$$

$$= \frac{\overset{4}{\cancel{16}}}{5} \times \frac{9}{\underset{1}{\cancel{4}}}$$

$$= \frac{4 \times 9}{5 \times 1}$$

$$= \frac{36}{5}$$

$$= 7\frac{1}{5}$$

Example 2:

$$2\frac{1}{4} \div 1\frac{1}{5}$$

$$= \frac{9}{4} \div \frac{6}{5}$$

$$= \frac{\overset{3}{\cancel{9}}}{4} \times \frac{5}{\underset{2}{\cancel{6}}}$$

$$= \frac{3 \times 5}{4 \times 2}$$

$$= \frac{15}{8}$$

$$= 1\frac{7}{8}$$

1.8 PERCENTAGES

For the non-calculator paper, you must be able to carry out some percentage calculations without using a calculator (see Section 1.5). Section 1.8.2 shows you examples using the non-calculator methods. However these methods only work easily with simple values.

In the rest of this book, the **decimal equivalent method** is used as the main approach for calculating percentages. This requires knowing the equivalent decimal and percentage forms, and then makes use of a calculator.

eg $\quad 27\% \leftrightarrow 0.27 \qquad 3\% \leftrightarrow 0.03 \qquad 17.5\% \leftrightarrow 0.175 \qquad 150\% \leftrightarrow 1.5$

Alternative methods of working with percentages, eg the non-calculator methods or using the % button on a calculator can also be used whenever a percentage calculation is required.

1.8.1 Equivalence of Fractions, Decimals and Percentages

Change from a fraction to a decimal by dividing the numerator by the denominator.

eg $\dfrac{3}{4} = 3 \div 4 = 0.75$

Change from a decimal to a fraction by setting it up as a fraction and simplifying.

eg $0.75 = \dfrac{\cancel{75}^3}{\cancel{100}_4} = \dfrac{3}{4}$

Change from a decimal to a percentage by changing to the percentage equivalent, or multiplying by 100.

eg $0.75 = 75\%$ (0.75×100)

Change from a percentage to decimal by changing to the decimal equivalent, or dividing by 100.

eg $75\% = 0.75$ $(75 \div 100)$

Change from a percentage to a fraction by writing as a fraction out of 100 and simplifying.

eg $75\% = \dfrac{\cancel{75}^3}{\cancel{100}_4} = \dfrac{3}{4}$

Change from a fraction to a percentage by changing to a decimal first or multiplying by 100.

eg $\begin{cases} \dfrac{3}{4} = 3 \div 4 = 0.75 = 75\% \\ \dfrac{3}{4} = \dfrac{3}{4} \times 100 = 75\% \end{cases}$

1.8.2 Non-Calculator Methods for Percentages

You can find a percentage of a quantity without using a calculator by changing to common fractions and simplifying (see Section 1.7).

Example 1: Find 70% of 8 kg.

$$70\% \text{ of } 8 \text{ kg} = \frac{\cancel{70}^7}{\cancel{100}_{10}} \times 8$$

$$= \frac{7}{\cancel{10}_5} \times \cancel{8}^4$$

$$= \frac{28}{5}$$

$$= 5\frac{3}{5} \text{ kg}$$

When you require to find a percentage which is a multiple or fraction of 10, it can be easier to find 10% first by dividing by 10.

You can also find 1% first by dividing by 100.

Example 2: Find 5% of £35.00.

By finding 10% first:		By finding 1% first:	
10% of £35.00 = £3.50	(÷10)	1% of £35.00 = £0.35	(÷100)
5% of £35.00 = **£1.75**	(÷2)	5% of £35.00 = **£1.75**	(×5)

For some common percentages, it is best to know and use the equivalent fraction.

Example 3: Find $33\frac{1}{3}$% of £1500.

$$33\frac{1}{3}\% \text{ of } £1500 = \frac{1}{3} \text{ of } £1500$$
$$= \frac{1500}{3}$$
$$= \textbf{£500}$$

1.8.3 Finding a Percentage of a Quantity (by Calculator)

The following examples show the decimal equivalent method. The percentage is changed to its decimal equivalent and multiplied against the quantity by calculator.

Example: Find (a) 35% of 460, (b) 3.5% of 460.

(a) 35% of 460
$$= 0.35 \times 460 = \textbf{161}$$

(b) 3.5% of 460
$$= 0.035 \times 460 = \textbf{16.1}$$

See Section 2.3.3 for percentage increases or decreases.

1.8.4 Finding One Quantity, a, as a Percentage of Another, b

1. Set up a over b as a fraction.

2. Change to the decimal equivalent.

3. Change to the percentage equivalent.

Example: What percentage of 1625 is 455?

(This means finding 455 <u>as a percentage of</u> 1625.)

$$\frac{455}{1625} = 0.28 = \textbf{28}\%$$

1.9 RATIO

A **ratio** is a way of comparing the relative sizes of quantities. It can be written in various forms.

eg　　　3 to 1　　or　　3:1　　or　　$\dfrac{3}{1}$

1.9.1 Splitting a Quantity in a Given Ratio (simple unitary ratios, ie 1 : ... or ... : 1)

1. Find the total number of "parts" in the ratio.

2. Divide the quantity by the number of parts to find the amount in each part.

3. Multiply the amount in one part by the number of parts in each share.

Example: In a will, £6000 is to be split between 2 relatives in the ratio 3:1. How much will each get?

Number of parts in the ratio $3:1 = 3 + 1 = 4$
Amount in each part = £6000 ÷ 4 = £1500

The **first relative** will get 3 x £1500 = **£4500**.
The **second relative** will get 1 x £1500 = **£1500**.

1.9.2 Splitting Quantities in a Given Ratio (more complex ratios)

The ratios allowed at this level can be more complicated, but are dealt with in the same manner as above.

eg　　　3:7　　or　　2:3　　or　　2:3:5

Example: In a will, £6000 is to be split between 3 relatives in the ratio 5:3:4. How much will each get?

Number of parts in the ratio $5:3:4 = 5 + 3 + 4 = 12$
Amount in each part = £6000 ÷ 12 = £500

The **first relative** will get 5 x £500 = **£2500**.
The **second relative** will get 3 x £500 = **£1500**.
The **third relative** will get 4 x £500 = **£2000**.

1.10 DISTANCE, SPEED AND TIME

You must know the formulae

$$D = S \times T \quad S = \frac{D}{T} \quad T = \frac{D}{S}$$

or use the triangle below to find them.

Remember that the letters come in alphabetical order!

Cover up the quantity that you wish to calculate.
The operation required to obtain it is shown.

You must work with hours and minutes as hours in decimal form.

eg

4 hrs 24 mins = $4\frac{24}{60}$ hrs = 4.4 hrs

0.15 hrs = 0.15 × 60 mins = 9 mins
so   2.15 hrs = 2 hrs 9 mins

Example: A man travelled 240 miles in 2 hrs 45 mins. What was his average speed?

$$2 \text{ hrs } 45 \text{ mins} = 2\frac{45}{60} \text{ hrs} = 2.75 \text{ hrs}$$

$$S = \frac{D}{T} = \frac{240}{2.75} = 87.27... = \textbf{87.3 mph} \text{ to 1 dp}$$

1.11 INDEX NOTATION

1.11.1 Index Notation (whole numbers)

5^4 is read as "5 (raised) to the power 4", and means $5 \times 5 \times 5 \times 5$.

1.11.2 Index Notation (rational numbers)

A fraction power indicates a root.

eg $8^{\frac{1}{3}} = \sqrt[3]{8} = 2$

See Section 6.11 (Indices) for further details.

1.12 SCIENTIFIC NOTATION

Any number can be written in **scientific notation** or **standard form**.
It is useful for writing very large or very small numbers.

1.12.1 Changing Numbers into Scientific Notation

In scientific notation, numbers are written in the form:

$$a \times 10^n \quad \text{where} \quad 1 \leq a < 10$$

1. To find a, write the significant digits in the number with 1 non-zero digit in front of the decimal point (a must be greater than or equal to 1 and less than 10).

2. n is given by the number of places each digit has moved past the decimal point when changing from the original form to a.
   In practice, it is easier to imagine the decimal point has moved. Count how many places the point has moved from where it was in the original number to where it is in a:
   - **positive** to the **left**   or remember   - **positive** for **big** numbers,
   - **negative** to the **right**,   - **negative** for **small** numbers.

eg

$$35\,600 = 3.56 \times 10^4$$

ie the point "moves" 4 places to the <u>left</u> in changing 35 600 into 3.56, so the power is 4.

$$0.000\,003\,91 = 3.91 \times 10^{-6}$$

ie the point "moves" 6 places to the <u>right</u> in changing 0.000 003 91 into 3.91, so the power is –6.

For changing from scientific notation to normal number form, reverse this process.

1.12.2 Using a Calculator for Scientific Notation

To enter 35 600 into a calculator in scientific notation form, enter 3.56, press the EXP button (or its equivalent), then enter 4.

On many calculators, scientific notation appears on the screen in the form
$$3.56 \quad ^{04}$$
Do not write it like this - you must remember to write it with the power of 10.

On some calculators, it is possible to set the calculator to convert numbers into scientific notation when you enter them as ordinary numbers.

1.12.3 Rounding in Scientific Notation

C/G

If a number in scientific form requires to be rounded, you round the a part to the required number of significant figures.

eg $\qquad 46\,855\,123 = 4.685\,512\,3 \times 10^7 = 4.7 \times 10^7$ to 2 sf

$\qquad 739\,522 = 7.395\,22 \times 10^5 = 7.40 \times 10^5$ to 3 sf

Note that in scientific form, every digit in the a part will be significant.

1.12.4 Calculations Using Scientific Notation

C/G

You can multiply and divide numbers in scientific notation on a calculator by entering them as in 1.12.2, and multiplying or dividing in the normal way.

Example: The speed of light is 3×10^8 m/s.

(a) How far will light travel in 1 year, ie what distance is 1 light year?

The nearest star Alpha Centauri is 4.29 light years away.

(b) How far is this in kilometres? Give your answer in scientific notation correct to 2 significant figures.

(a) $S = 3 \times 10^8$ m/s

$\quad = 3 \times 10^8 \times 60 \times 60 \times 24 \times 365$ m/yr

$\quad = 9.460\,8 \times 10^{15}$ m/yr

$\quad = 9.460\,8 \times 10^{15} \div 1000$ km/yr

$\quad = \mathbf{9.460\,8 \times 10^{12}}$ **km/yr**

Light travels $\mathbf{9.460\,8 \times 10^{12}}$ **km** in 1 year.

(b) $D = S \times T = 9.460\,8 \times 10^{12} \times 4.29$

$\quad = 4.058\,6... \times 10^{13}$

$\quad = \mathbf{4.1 \times 10^{13}}$ **km** to 2 sf

1.13 SURDS

A **surd** is a root which has an irrational value,

eg $\sqrt{5}$ $\sqrt{65}$ $\sqrt[3]{23}$

but not a root which has a rational value.

eg $\sqrt{9}=3$ $\sqrt{6.25}=2.5$ $\sqrt[3]{27}=3$ $\sqrt{\dfrac{4}{25}}=\dfrac{2}{5}$

1.13.1 Basic Rules

C

Most of the work with surds makes use of one of these two basic rules:

$$\sqrt{ab}=\sqrt{a}\sqrt{b} \qquad \sqrt{\dfrac{a}{b}}=\dfrac{\sqrt{a}}{\sqrt{b}}$$

1.13.2 Simplifying Surds

C

1. Break the number into factors, one of which is a perfect square.

2. Apply the basic rules to simplify the surd, as far as possible.

eg $\sqrt{75}=\sqrt{25\times3}=\sqrt{25}\times\sqrt{3}=5\sqrt{3}$

$$\sqrt{\dfrac{18}{5}}=\dfrac{\sqrt{18}}{\sqrt{5}}=\dfrac{\sqrt{9\times2}}{\sqrt{5}}=\dfrac{\sqrt{9}\times\sqrt{2}}{\sqrt{5}}=\dfrac{3\sqrt{2}}{\sqrt{5}}$$

1.13.3 Adding and Subtracting Surds

C

Multiples of the same surd can be added and subtracted as in normal algebra.

eg $3\sqrt{5}+2\sqrt{2}+\sqrt{5}-5\sqrt{2}$
$=4\sqrt{5}-3\sqrt{2}$

1.13.4 Multiplying Surds

1. Multiply out any brackets by normal algebraic methods.

2. Combine the surds by using the first rule in reverse.

eg $\quad \sqrt{2} \times \sqrt{6} = \sqrt{2 \times 6} = \sqrt{12}$

3. Simplify as before.

Example: Simplify $(\sqrt{2} + \sqrt{3})^2$.

$$
\begin{aligned}
(\sqrt{2} + \sqrt{3})^2 &= (\sqrt{2} + \sqrt{3})(\sqrt{2} + \sqrt{3}) \\
&= \sqrt{2}\sqrt{2} + \sqrt{2}\sqrt{3} + \sqrt{3}\sqrt{2} + \sqrt{3}\sqrt{3} \\
&= \sqrt{4} + \sqrt{6} + \sqrt{6} + \sqrt{9} \\
&= 2 + 2\sqrt{6} + 3 \\
&= \mathbf{5 + 2\sqrt{6}}
\end{aligned}
$$

1.13.5 Rationalising a Denominator

It is often thought to be neater to avoid leaving an irrational value in the denominator of a fraction.

Multiply the numerator and the denominator of the fraction by the surd value in the denominator.

Example 1:

$$
\begin{aligned}
\frac{3}{\sqrt{5}} &= \frac{3}{\sqrt{5}} \times \frac{\sqrt{5}}{\sqrt{5}} \\
&= \frac{3\sqrt{5}}{\sqrt{25}} \\
&= \frac{3\sqrt{5}}{5}
\end{aligned}
$$

Example 2:

$$
\begin{aligned}
\frac{\sqrt{3}+1}{2\sqrt{3}} &= \frac{(\sqrt{3}+1)}{2\sqrt{3}} \times \frac{\sqrt{3}}{\sqrt{3}} \\
&= \frac{\sqrt{3}\sqrt{3} + \sqrt{3}}{2\sqrt{3}\sqrt{3}} \\
&= \frac{\sqrt{9} + \sqrt{3}}{2 \times \sqrt{9}} \\
&= \frac{3 + \sqrt{3}}{6}
\end{aligned}
$$

2. MONEY

For most of the money topics, you should be familiar with the terms and the general methods used. The details, eg interest rate, rate of income tax, etc, would be supplied if required in a question.

2.1 EARNINGS

Most earnings are paid weekly (**wage**) or monthly (**salary**).

The total amount (**gross pay**) usually consists of a basic amount **(basic pay)** plus any **additions**.

eg **bonus** - An extra payment, possibly for meeting some target.

    overtime - A payment for any hours worked beyond the basic contract. These are often paid at a higher rate, eg **double time** (2 x basic rate per hour), **time and a half** (1.5 x basic rate per hour), etc.

    commission - An extra payment based on, for example, the amount of sales.

From the gross pay, various **deductions** are made to leave the **net pay**.

eg **National Insurance** contributions - An amount deducted by the employer to go towards paying for services like the health service, benefits, etc. It is normally calculated as a percentage of the salary.

    superannuation - A payment towards a pension scheme. It is normally calculated as a percentage of the salary.

    Income Tax - An amount deducted by the employer to go to the government. Each individual is allowed some of their salary tax-free (their **allowances**). Out of the remainder of their salary (**taxable income**), they then pay a percentage as **income tax**. There are different percentage rates depending on the size of their taxable income.

2.2 INTEREST

Interest is paid out on money invested. It is also charged on money borrowed.

The basic sum of money is called the **principal**.

The interest is calculated as a percentage of the principal using the **interest rate**. This is normally given as an annual percentage, eg **5% pa** (per annum).

The total of principal plus interest is called the **amount**.

G

2.2.1 Simple Interest

The principal remains unchanged from year to year.

Example 1: Calculate the simple interest on £350 for 2 years at 6.5% pa.

Annual interest = 6.5% of £350
$$= 0.065 \times £350 = £22.75$$
2 years interest = $2 \times 22.75 = $ **£45.50**

Example 2: Calculate the simple interest on £350 for 8 months at 6.5% pa.

Annual interest = £22.75 (as above)

8 months interest $= \dfrac{8}{12}$ of £22.75

$$= 0.66... \times £22.75$$

$$= £15.17 \quad \text{to the nearest penny.}$$

C/G

2.2.2 Compound Interest

The interest is added on to the principal each year to create a new principal. Banks will normally give compound interest.

Example: Calculate the compound interest on £350 for 2 years at 6.5% pa.

1st principal		= £350
1st interest	= 6.5% of £350	
	= 0.065 × £350	= £22.75
2nd principal	= £350 + £22.75	= £372.75
2nd interest	= 6.5% of £372 *	
	= 0.065 × £372	= £24.18
Total interest	= £22.75 + £24.18	= **£46.93**

* Banks may calculate interest on complete pounds only.
  Specific procedures like this would be given in a question.

2.3 EXPENDITURE

2.3.1 Insurance Premiums   **G**

The **premium** is the amount paid, usually monthly or annually, for the **policy**.
It is normally given as a rate per £100 or £1000. Use proportion methods.

Example: Find the premium for a House Contents policy covering £2250 at £3.50
per £100.

$$
\begin{array}{ccc}
\text{amount} & & \text{premium} \\
100 & \to & 3.50 \\
2250 & \to & \dfrac{2250}{100} \times 3.50 = 78.75 \quad \text{The premium is } \textbf{£78.75}.
\end{array}
$$

2.3.2 Foreign Exchange   **G**

The **rate of exchange** for each currency will normally be given by an amount
per £. Use proportion methods to answer questions of this kind.

Example: A man changes £150 into French francs at an exchange rate of
9.83 F to the £.
(a) How many francs does he receive?

He then changes 200 francs back into sterling at a rate of 9.75 F to the £.
(b) How much does he receive?

(a)

$$
\begin{array}{ccc}
£ & & \text{francs} \\
1 & \to & 9.83 \\
150 & \to & \dfrac{150}{1} \times 9.83 \\
& & = 1474.50
\end{array}
$$

(b)

$$
\begin{array}{ccc}
\text{francs} & & £ \\
9.75 & \to & 1 \\
200 & \to & \dfrac{200}{9.75} \times 1 \\
& & = 20.51
\end{array}
$$

He receives **1474.50 francs**.   He receives **£20.51**.

2.3.3 Appreciation/Depreciation   **C/G**

An item can increase in its value over a period of time (**appreciate**) or decrease in
its value (**depreciate**). This is often given by a percentage rate.

The methods used are the same as for compound interest, although depreciation
involves subtracting an amount.

Example: A car loses 25% of its value over the first year and 20% over the second year. What would a car costing £12 500 be worth at the end of 2 years?

Original value $= £12\,500$

1st depreciation $= 25\%$ of £12 500
                     $= 0.25 \times £12\,500 = £3125$
Value after 1 year $= £12\,500 - £3125 = £9375$

2nd depreciation $= 20\%$ of £9375
                     $= 0.20 \times £9375 = £1875$
Value after 2 years $= £9375 - £1875$
                     $= £7500$

Alternative Method:

When using the decimal equivalent method, a percentage increase or decrease can be calculated directly.

eg   A 25% increase has a decimal equivalent of 1.25.

       A 25% decrease has a decimal equivalent of 0.75.

Example: What is the value of the car after the first year in the above example?

Value after 1 year = 75% of £12 500 = **£9375**

2.4 BORROWING

2.4.1 Loans

G

When money is borrowed, you have to pay interest to the lender as well as repaying the principal. The methods used are the same as those for calculating interest when investing money.

Example: A man borrows £4500 for one year from a bank offering an interest rate of 14.9% pa. How much will the loan cost him altogether?

Loan $= £4500$
Interest $= 14.9\%$ of £4500
                    $= 0.149 \times £4500$ $= £670.50$
Total cost of loan $= £5170.50$

2.4.2 Hire Purchase (HP)

This is a method of purchasing goods and paying for them over a period of time.
It normally involves paying a **deposit** (often a percentage of the basic cost)
followed by a series of regular **instalments**.
You will often pay more in total than the basic cost.

Example: A hifi system costs £450 cash or can be bought on HP with a 20%
deposit and 6 monthly instalments of £69.
How much more does it cost to buy on HP?

Deposit = 20% of £450 = 0.20 x £450 = £90
Cost of instalments = 6 x £69 = £414
Total cost by HP = £90 + £414 = £504
Extra cost by HP = £504 − £450 = **£54**

2.5 SURCHARGES

2.5.1 Discount

A **discount** can be given as a cash amount or a percentage, and is subtracted
from the total.

2.5.2 VAT

Value added tax (VAT) is the tax included in the cost of most items you buy.
The rate is set by the Government and is currently (2000) 17.5% for most items.

2.5.3 Calculating the Basic Price Before VAT

Use proportion methods, taking the total cost as 117.5%, ie the cost before VAT
plus 17.5%, and then find what 100% would be.

Example: A lady paid £449.99 for a hifi. What was the cost before VAT?

$$
\begin{array}{ccc}
\% & & £ \\
117.5 & \rightarrow & 449.99 \\
100 & \rightarrow & \dfrac{100}{117.5} \times 449.99 \\
& & = 382.97 \quad \text{to the nearest penny.}
\end{array}
$$

The hifi cost **£382.97** before VAT.

3. MEASURE

3.1 UNITS

G

You should know all the basic units and their relationships with each other.

Length

$$10\ mm = 1\ cm \qquad 100\ cm = 1000\ mm = 1\ m \qquad 1000\ m = 1\ km$$

Mass (Weight)

$$1000\ g = 1\ kg \qquad 1000\ kg = 1\ tonne$$

Volume

$$1000\ ml = 1\ l \qquad 10\ ml = 1\ cl\ \text{(centilitre)}$$
$$1\ cm^3 = 1\ ml \qquad 1000\ cm^3 = 1\ l \qquad 1000\ l = 1\ m^3$$

3.2 CONVERSION OF UNITS (AREA / VOLUME)

C/G

Be careful when working with square or cubic units.

eg $1\ m^2 = 100 \times 100 = 10\ 000\ cm^2$ $1\ m^3 = 100 \times 100 \times 100 = 1\ 000\ 000\ cm^3$

1 *hectare* = 10 000 m^2

3.3 TOLERANCE

G

In practice, it is not possible to make an exact measurement. To allow for that, a **tolerance** on a measurement may be given, providing a range of acceptable values. It will normally be written in the form ... $\pm$ ... , eg 25 ± 2 .

Example: An angle has to be drawn to $(25 \pm 2)°$.

Which of the following would be acceptable?

$26.3°$ $22.9°$ $23°$ $27.4°$ $25°$

Minimum acceptable = $25 - 2 = 23°$

Maximum acceptable = $25 + 2 = 27°$

So **26.3°**, **23°** and **25°** are acceptable.

4. SHAPE

4.1 ANGLES

4.1.1 Definitions and Terminology

An angle is a measure of the size of a turn.
Angles are usually measured in degrees (°), and 360° make up one full turn.

An angle can also measure how 2 lines meet. The meeting point is called the **vertex** or corner and the lines are called the **arms** of the angle.

4.1.2 Naming an Angle

You name points using capital letters, eg A, B, etc.

The line joining A to B is named AB.

The angle formed by the line AB meeting the line BC is named the angle ABC or CBA.

The vertex is always the middle letter.

4.1.3 Types of Angles

acute	right	obtuse	straight	reflex

$x < 90°$ $x = 90°$ $90° < x < 180°$ $x = 180°$ $180° < x < 360°$

4.1.4 Special Angles

supplementary angles	complementary angles	(vertically) opposite angles

 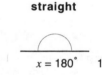

$x° + y° = 180°$ $x° + y° = 90°$

x is called the **supplement** of y x is called the **complement** of y opposite angles are equal

Angles with Parallel Lines

corresponding (F-) angles are equal

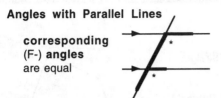

alternate (Z-) angles are equal

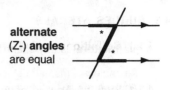

4.2 TRIANGLES

4.2.1 Special Types of Triangles (G)

Isosceles

2 equal sides
2 equal angles
1 axis of symmetry

Equilateral

3 equal sides
3 equal angles
3 axes of symmetry

Scalene

all sides different
all angles different
no axes of symmetry

4.2.2 Triangle Results (G)

Sum of angles
$x° + y° + z° = 180°$

Area of triangle $= \frac{1}{2}bh$
(b is the base,
h is the perpendicular height)

4.2.3 Special Lines in a Triangle (C/G)

A line from the mid point of a side to the opposite vertex is called a **median**.

A line from a vertex which meets the opposite side at right-angles is called an **altitude**. It is used to give the **perpendicular height** of a triangle.

A line which passes through the mid-point of a side at right-angles to the side is called a **perpendicular bisector**.

median

altitude

perpendicular bisector

Lines which meet at the same point are said to be **concurrent**.
Points which lie on the same straight line are said to be **collinear**.

4.3 QUADRILATERALS Ⓖ

A **quadrilateral** is any shape with 4 straight sides.

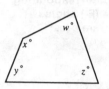

4.3.1 Sum of Angles of a Quadrilateral

$$w° + x° + y° + z° = 360°$$

4.3.2 Basic Properties of Common Quadrilaterals Ⓖ
- sides, angles, symmetry, diagonals (d), perimeter (P) and area (A)

Square

4 equal sides
4 equal angles (90°)
4 axes of symmetry
rotation symmetry of
    order 4
equal diagonals bisect
    each other at 90°

$$P = 4l \qquad A = l^2$$

Rectangle

opposite sides equal
4 equal angles (90°)
2 axes of symmetry
rotation symmetry of
    order 2
equal diagonals
    bisect each other

$$P = 2l + 2b \qquad A = lb$$

Rhombus

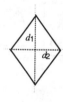

4 equal sides
opposite angles equal
2 axes of symmetry
rotation symmetry of
    order 2
diagonals bisect each
    other at 90°

$$A = \frac{1}{2}d_1 d_2$$

Kite

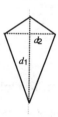

2 pairs of equal sides
    (adjacent)
1 pair of equal
    angles (opposite)
1 axis of symmetry
no rotation symmetry
one diagonal bisects
    the other at 90°

$$A = \frac{1}{2}d_1 d_2$$

Parallelogram

opposite sides equal
    and parallel
opposite angles equal
no axes of symmetry
rotation symmetry of
    order 2

$$A = bh$$

Trapezium

1 pair of parallel
    sides
no equal angles
no axes of symmetry
no rotation symmetry

$$A = \frac{1}{2}(b_1 + b_2)h$$

4.4 POLYGONS

Any shape with all its sides straight is called a **polygon**,

eg **pentagon** (5 sides), **hexagon** (6), **octagon** (8), **decagon** (10).

If all the sides <u>and</u> all the angles are equal, it is said to be **regular**.

4.5 CIRCLES

The perimeter of a circle is called the **circumference** (C).
Every point on the circumference is **equidistant** (the same distance) from the centre of the circle.

Any straight line joining the centre to a point on the circumference is called a **radius** (r).

Any straight line joining two points on the circumference and passing through the centre is called a **diameter** (d).

$d = 2r$	$C = \pi d$ or $C = 2\pi r$	$A = \pi r^2$	$\pi = \dfrac{C}{d}$

π is the exact value obtained when the circumference of any circle is divided by the diameter. It is an irrational number, with an infinite decimal expansion 3.141 592 65...

It can be approximated for calculations, eg 3.14 to 3 sf, but for calculations using a calculator, use the π button and round the final answer as appropriate.

Example: Find the area of a circle with circumference 135 cm correct to 3 sf.

$C = \pi d$

$135 = \pi d$

$d = \dfrac{135}{\pi} = 42.97...$

$r = \dfrac{d}{2} = 21.48...$

$A = \pi r^2 = \pi \times 21.48...^2$

$= 1450.2...$

$= \mathbf{1450\ cm^2}$ to 3 sf

Note: An elongated circle is called an **ellipse**.

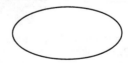

4.6 THREE DIMENSIONAL (3D) SOLIDS

4.6.1 Net of a Solid

A **net** of a 3D solid is a arrangement of the faces that
could be folded to create a model of the solid.
For example, a possible net for a cube:

4.6.2 Volumes (V) and Surface Areas (SA) of Common Solids

Cube

$$V = l^3 \qquad SA = 6l^2$$

Cuboid

$$V = lbh \qquad SA = 2lb + 2bh + 2lh$$

**Prism †
(Triangular)**

$$V = Ah \qquad SA = 2A + 3 \text{ sides } (rectangles)$$

where A is the area of the
(triangular) cross-section

Cylinder

$$V = \pi r^2 h \qquad SA = 2\pi r^2 + 2\pi rh$$

This formula for SA is for a <u>closed</u>
cylinder with a top and base.

Pyramid *

$$V = \frac{1}{3}Ah \qquad SA = A + \text{ sides } (triangles)$$

where A is area of base and h is
perpendicular height of the pyramid

Cone *

$$V = \frac{1}{3}\pi r^2 h \qquad SA = \pi r^2 + \pi rs$$

where s is the slant height

$$s = \sqrt{r^2 + h^2}$$

Sphere *

and h is the perpendicular height

$$V = \frac{4}{3}\pi r^3 \qquad SA = 4\pi r^2$$

* The formulae for pyramids, cones and spheres are not required for Standard
Grade, although the shapes should be known. Some of the formulae are given
on the formula list in the **General** exam but not in the **Credit** exam.

† A **prism** is any solid whose **cross-section** at all points along the length of the shape is **congruent** (the same size and shape, see Section 4.12.2).
If the ends are perpendicular to the sides, it is called a **right** prism.

Only a **triangular prism** is specifically mentioned in the syllabus.

Example 1: A closed cylindrical tin of volume 6260 cm3 has radius 15 cm.
What is its surface area?

First use the volume to find the height.

$$V = \pi r^2 h$$
$$6260 = \pi \times 15^2 \times h$$
$$h = \frac{6260}{\pi \times 15^2} = 8.85...$$

$$SA = 2\pi r^2 + 2\pi rh$$
$$= 2\pi \times 15^2 + 2\pi \times 15 \times 8.85...$$
$$= 2248.3...$$
$$= \textbf{2250 cm}^\textbf{2} \text{ to 3 sf}$$

Example 2: A cone and a sphere have the same radius and volume.
Find a relationship between the height and the radius of the cone.

Volume of cone = Volume of sphere

Since both have the same r,

$$\frac{1}{3}\pi r^2 h = \frac{4}{3}\pi r^3$$
$$\pi r^2 h = 4\pi r^3$$
$$r^2 h = 4r^3$$
$$h = 4r$$

The height is 4 times the radius.

4.7 COORDINATES AND STRAIGHT LINES

4.7.1 Basic Coordinates

The coordinate system uses a horizontal line (*x*-**axis**) and a vertical line (*y*-**axis**), each with a scale. Negative values can be included if necessary.

Each point is referenced by a pair of coordinates giving two numbers, (*across, up*).

The point (0,0) is called the **origin (O)**.

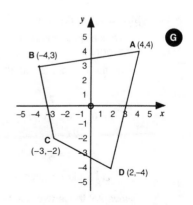

Coordinates link geometry (the study of shape) with the powerful methods of algebra.

Every shape, eg a straight line, a parabola, etc, can be regarded as a set of points. If you can find a rule (equation) linking the x- and y- coordinates of every point in that shape, you call it **the equation of the shape**.

You often find that similar shapes will have similar equations.

4.7.2 The Equation of a Straight Line

G

> A **vertical** line has an equation of the form $x = c$.
> A **horizontal** line has an equation of the form $y = d$.

> All other straight lines have an equation of the form $y = ax + b$, and every equation of this form will produce a straight line.

Example 1: Draw the line with equation $y = 2x - 1$.

First choose some x-values (at least 3).
eg $x = -2, 0, 2$

Make a table and find the corresponding
y-values using the equation.

eg $x = -2$ $y = 2 \times (-2) - 1 = -5$

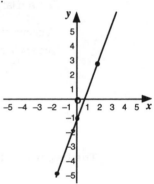

x	-2	0	2
y	-5	-1	3

Plot the points, and draw a line through them.

Alternative Method:

This is a quick method which will work as long as the line does not pass through the origin.

Find the intercepts with the x- and y-axes, by setting $y = 0$ and $x = 0$.

$$y = 2x - 1$$
$$y = 0, \quad 0 = 2x - 1$$
$$2x = 1$$
$$x = \tfrac{1}{2}$$
$(\tfrac{1}{2}, 0)$ is x intercept.

$$y = 2x - 1$$
$$x = 0, \quad y = 2 \times 0 - 1$$
$$y = -1$$
$(0, -1)$ is y intercept.

Now plot these two points and draw the line through them.

Example 2: If the points with coordinates $(7, a)$ and $(b, 20)$ lie on the line with equation $y = 2x - 3$, what are the values of a and b?

$$y = 2x - 3$$
$$x = 7, \; y = a$$
$$a = 2 \times 7 - 3$$
$$a = 11$$

$$y = 2x - 3$$
$$x = b, \; y = 20$$
$$20 = 2b - 3$$
$$2b = 23$$
$$b = 11\tfrac{1}{2}$$

4.7.3 The Gradient of a Line

C/G

The gradient of a line is a number which measures the steepness of the slope. It is given by:

$$m = \frac{y}{x} = \frac{vertical}{horizontal} = \frac{rise}{run}$$

The gradient of the line joining $A\,(x_A, y_A)$ to $B\,(x_B, y_B)$ is given by:

$$m_{AB} = \frac{y_B - y_A}{x_B - x_A}$$

Lines with a **positive** gradient slope **up** to the right.

Lines with a **negative** gradient slope **down** the right.

The larger the number "value", ie the more positive or the more negative, the steeper the line.

The gradient of a vertical line is said to be **undefined**.

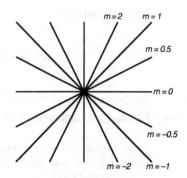

4.7.4 The Equation $y = mx + c$.

C/G

> When the equation of a straight line is written in the form
>
> $$y = mx + c,$$
>
> the value m gives the **gradient** of the line,
> and the value c gives the y-**intercept**.

This allows a very quick method of sketching a straight line.

1. Rearrange the equation into $y = mx + c$ form.

2. Mark the y intercept on the diagram.

3. Use the gradient to find a series of other points on the line.

   For example, for a gradient of $\dfrac{y}{x}$, go x along horizontally, and y up vertically
   to find the next point, and then repeat it from there to find another.

Note: If the gradient is negative, assign the negative to the y value and go
<u>down</u> y for x along horizontally. (See the example below.)

Example: Sketch the line with equation $2x + 3y = 9$.

$$2x + 3y = 9$$
$$3y = -2x + 9$$
$$y = -\tfrac{2}{3}x + 3$$

$m = -\tfrac{2}{3}$, $\quad y$ intercept (0,3).

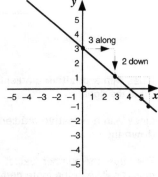

Plot the point (0,3).

$$m = \frac{y}{x} = \frac{-2}{3} \quad \text{ie 2 down for 3 along}$$

Go 3 along, down 2 and plot (3,1).

Plot another point and draw a line through the points.

Note: If you only require a rough sketch of the line, it is not necessary to carry
out Step 3 in detail - just estimate the steepness of the line from its
gradient.

4.8 SYMMETRY

4.8.1 Bilateral or Line Symmetry

A shape is said to have **bilateral** or **line symmetry** if one side of it is a mirror image of the other side about a line.

Each such line in a shape is called a **line** or **axis of symmetry**.

For example, an equilateral triangle has 3 axes of symmetry.

4.8.2 Rotational Symmetry

A shape is said to have **rotational symmetry** if it can fit its outline in more than 1 way when it is turned around.

If it can fit its outline in n different ways, it is said to have **rotational symmetry of order n**.

For example, an equilateral triangle has rotational symmetry of order 3.

Rotational symmetry of order 2 is called **half-turn symmetry**.

Note: The use of the term **order** is not specified in the Standard Grade syllabus, although it is useful for describing the symmetry.

4.9 PYTHAGORAS' THEOREM

In any right angled triangle, the longest side (opposite the right angle) is called the **hypotenuse**.

When naming a triangle, you use the small letter corresponding to the capital letter used for the opposite vertex. For example, the side opposite vertex A is named a.

4.9.1 Pythagoras' Theorem

For the right angled triangle ABC, with the right angle at A:

$$a^2 = b^2 + c^2$$

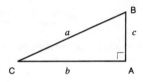

Example 1 (finding a hypotenuse):

In the diagram below, find x.

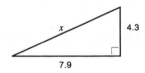

By Pythagoras' Theorem,

$$x^2 = 4.3^2 + 7.9^2$$
$$x^2 = 80.9$$
$$x = \sqrt{80.9}$$
$$= 8.99...$$
$$= \mathbf{9.0} \text{ to 1dp}$$

Example 2 (finding another side):

In the diagram below, find x.

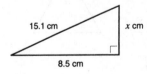

By Pythagoras' Theorem,

$$15.1^2 = x^2 + 8.5^2$$
$$x^2 = 15.1^2 - 8.5^2$$
$$x^2 = 155.76$$
$$x = \sqrt{155.76}$$
$$= 12.48...$$
$$= \mathbf{12.5 \text{ cm}} \text{ to 1dp}$$

Note: Do not include the units in the working, only in the final answer.

G

4.9.2 Finding the Distance Between Points

Pythagoras' Theorem can be used to calculate the distance between 2 points, given the coordinates.

Example: Find the distance between A (–4,3) and B (3,–2).

1. Sketch the points on a set of axes.

2. Complete a right angled triangle using the line AB as the hypotenuse, and taking the other sides, one horizontal and one vertical.

3. Calculate the length of the sides, and use Pythagoras' Theorem to find AB.

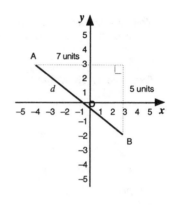

By Pythagoras' Theorem,

$$d^2 = 7^2 + 5^2$$

$$d^2 = 74$$

$$d = \sqrt{74}$$

$$= 8.60...$$

AB is **8.6 units** to 1dp.

Alternative Method:

The same result can be obtained by substituting the coordinates into **the distance formula.** The formula is not specifically mentioned in the syllabus.

$$d_{AB} = \sqrt{(x_B - x_A)^2 + (y_B - y_A)^2}$$

$$d_{AB} = \sqrt{(x_B - x_A)^2 + (y_B - y_A)^2}$$
$$= \sqrt{(3 - (-4))^2 + (-2 - 3)^2}$$
$$= \sqrt{(7)^2 + (-5)^2}$$
$$= \sqrt{49 + 25} = \sqrt{74}$$

AB is **8.6 units** to 1dp.

4.9.3 The Converse of Pythagoras' Theorem

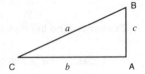

Pythagoras' Theorem can be used "in reverse" to decide whether a triangle is right angled.

> For any triangle, ABC, if $a^2 = b^2 + c^2$,
> then the triangle is right angled at A.

You must <u>show</u> that $a^2 = b^2 + c^2$, <u>not assume</u> it to be true.
It is important to set the working out properly.

Example 1: Show that triangle PQR below is right angled at Q.

$$PR^2 = 10.5^2 = 110.25$$

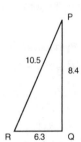

$$PQ^2 = 8.4^2 = 70.56$$
$$RQ^2 = 6.3^2 = 39.69$$
$$PQ^2 + RQ^2 = 110.25$$

$$PR^2 = PQ^2 + RQ^2$$

So by the Converse of Pythagoras' Theorem, triangle PQR is right angled at Q.

If a^2 is <u>not</u> equal to $b^2 + c^2$, then the triangle cannot be right angled.

Example 2: A flagpole of height 4.2 m is supported from the top by a wire support of length 5.2 m. If the support is fixed to a point on the ground 2.5 m away from the foot of the pole, will the pole be standing vertically?

First identify the triangle.
It helps to draw it separately and introduce letters.

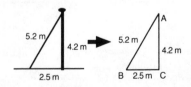

$$AB^2 = 5.2^2 = 27.04$$
$$AC^2 = 4.2^2 = 17.64 \quad BC^2 = 2.5^2 = 6.25$$
$$AC^2 + BC^2 = 23.89$$
$$AB^2 \neq AC^2 + BC^2$$

So triangle ABC is not right angled.
So the flagpole **cannot** be vertical.

4.10 CIRCLE RESULTS

4.10.1 Basic Terminology

major arc

major sector

minor sector

minor arc

major segment

chord

minor segment

Any 2 points on the circumference of a circle separate the circumference into 2 **arcs**.

When the 2 points are connected to the centre with radii, the circle is separated into 2 **sectors**.

A straight line joining any 2 points on the circumference is called a **chord**.
A chord separates the circle into 2 **segments**.

Note: In each case, we can distinguish one from the other by calling the larger the **major** arc / sector / segment, and the smaller the **minor** arc / sector / segment. The use of major and minor is not specified in the syllabus.

4.10.2 Tangent to a Circle

A **tangent** to a circle is a straight line which **touches** the circle at only one point P. The point P is called the **point of contact**.

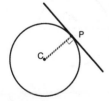

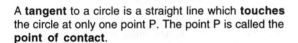

If a radius is drawn from the centre to the point of contact, then the tangent meets the radius at 90°.

The introduction of a right angle makes the use of either Pythagoras' Theorem or trigonometry the likely method of solution in problems.
A right-angled triangle must first be identified.

Example: A tangent to a circle centre C, radius 8.5 cm, meets the circle at P.
Q is a point on the tangent such that PQ is 15.3 cm.
What is the distance CQ?

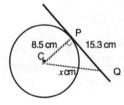

By Pythagoras' Theorem in the
right angled triangle CQP,

$$CQ^2 = CP^2 + PQ^2$$
$$x^2 = 8.5^2 + 15.3^2$$
$$= 306.34$$
$$x = \sqrt{306.34} = 17.50...$$

CQ is **17.5 cm** to 1dp.

4.10.3 Angles in a Semi-circle

(G)

An angle drawn from one end of a diameter to a point
on the circumference to the other end of the diameter
is called an **angle in a semi-circle**.

Any angle in a semi-circle is a right angle.

Again, the introduction of a right angle makes
Pythagoras' Theorem or trigonometry the likely
method of solution in problems.

Example: AB is the diameter of a circle, and has length 6.0 cm.
AP is a chord in the circle, such that angle BAP = 30°.
What is the length of chord AP?

Since AB is a diameter, $\angle APB = 90°$,
so $\triangle APB$ is right angled.

$$\cos 30° = \frac{adj}{hyp} = \frac{AP}{6.0}$$
$$6.0 \cos 30° = AP$$
$$AP = 5.19...$$
$$= \textbf{5.2 cm} \text{ to 1dp}$$

4.10.4 Angles, Arcs and Sectors

You can use either a ratio method or a multiplier method.
The example below has been done both ways.

Many of these questions are done by comparing an angle, arc or sector with the angle (360°), the circumference or the area of the whole circle.

For any circle:

$$\frac{\angle AOB}{360°} = \frac{arc\ AB}{circumference\ of\ circle} = \frac{sector\ AOB}{area\ of\ circle}$$

You will normally use 2 parts of the ratio.

Note: The angle AOB is said to be **subtended by** (standing on) the arc AB.

Example (using a ratio):

A and B are 2 points on the circumference of a circle of radius 10 cm. If angle AOB is 50°, what is the length of arc AB, and the area of sector AOB?

$$\frac{\angle AOB}{360°} = \frac{arc\ AB}{circumference\ of\ circle} = \frac{sector\ AOB}{area\ of\ circle}$$

$C = 2\pi r = 2\pi \times 10 = 62.8...$ $\qquad A = \pi r^2 = \pi \times 10^2 = 314.1...$

$$\frac{50}{360} = \frac{x}{62.8...} \qquad\qquad \frac{50}{360} = \frac{y}{314.1...}$$

$$\frac{x}{62.8...} = \frac{50}{360} \qquad\qquad \frac{y}{314.1...} = \frac{50}{360}$$

$$x = \frac{50}{360} \times 62.8... \qquad\qquad y = \frac{50}{360} \times 314.1...$$

$$= 8.72... \qquad\qquad\qquad = 43.63...$$

Arc AB is **8.7 cm** to 1 dp. $\qquad$ Sector AOB is **43.6 cm^2** to 1 dp.

Note: Some questions may require you to give the answer as an exact multiple of π.
For example, the circumference could have been given as 20π.
This is called the **exact value** of the circumference.

Using fractions, you then obtain an exact value for the arc AB of $\frac{25\pi}{9}$ cm.

Alternative Method (using a multiplier):

Find the fraction of the circle involved from one of the quantities, and calculate the other quantities using the fraction as a multiplier.

$$\angle AOB = \frac{50}{360} \text{ of the circle}$$

arc $AB = \dfrac{50}{360}$ of the circumference $\qquad$ sector $AOB = \dfrac{50}{360}$ of the circle area

$$= \frac{50}{360} \times 62.8... \qquad\qquad\qquad = \frac{50}{360} \times 314.1...$$

$$= 8.72... \qquad\qquad\qquad\qquad\quad = 43.63...$$

Arc AB is **8.7 cm** to 1 dp. $\qquad\qquad$ Sector AOB is **43.6 cm²** to 1 dp.

Note: You can also compare 2 angles, arcs or sectors with each other directly using a similar result.

For any circle:

$$\frac{\angle AOB}{\angle COD} = \frac{arc\ AB}{arc\ CD} = \frac{sector\ AOB}{sector\ COD}$$

4.10.5 Diameters and Chords

C

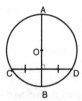

In a circle, if any two of the following statements are true,

1. AB is (or can be extended to be) a diameter,
2. AB bisects CD,
3. AB is perpendicular to CD,

then so is the third.

Note: Again, the introduction of a right angle makes Pythagoras' Theorem or trigonometry the likely method of solution in problems.

For example, a right angled triangle can be created by adding a radius, eg OD, or by adding a line, eg AD, to the above drawing.

Example: In a circle, centre C, of diameter 20 cm, M is the midpoint of a chord PQ. If CM = 5 cm, what is the length of the chord PQ?

1. Draw diameter AB passing through M.
   By the above result, AB is perpendicular to PQ.

2. Draw right angled triangle CMQ.

3. Use Pythagoras' Theorem.

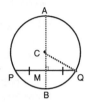

By Pythagoras' Theorem,

$$CQ^2 = MQ^2 + CM^2$$
$$10^2 = x^2 + 5^2$$
$$x^2 = 10^2 - 5^2 = 75$$
$$x = \sqrt{75} = 8.66...$$

So $PQ = 2 \times MQ$
$\quad = 2 \times 8.66...$
$\quad = $ **17.3 cm** to 1 dp

4.11 SCALE DRAWINGS

There is normally a question in the **General** paper which asks you to use a scale drawing. If you use any other method, you will receive <u>no</u> marks, even if you get the right answer!

A scale drawing can sometimes be used to solve an R&A question, unless the question states "do not use a scale drawing".

4.11.1 Scales

Scales can be expressed:

in words,	eg	1 cm represents 10 m,
as a ratio,	eg	1:1000,
using a scaled line,	eg	0m 10m 20m 30m 40m 50m ,
using the **Representative Fraction**,	eg	$\frac{1}{1000}$.

4.11.2 Using a Scale Drawing

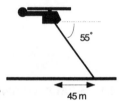

When using a scale drawing to answer a question:

1. If a scale is given, use it. If not, choose an appropriate scale.
   It must produce a drawing big enough to give sufficiently accurate answers.
   Choose a scale that will be easy to convert.

2. Show both the scale length and the actual length for each line.
   Show any working you use to change from one to the other.

3. Draw all lines as accurately as possible.
   You should be able to measure to the nearest mm.

4. Measure all angles as accurately as possible.
   You should be able to measure to the nearest degree.

Example: A helicopter is flying above some horizontal
ground. Its searchlight is aimed at an angle of
depression of 55°. The beam is shining on
the ground at a point 45 metres in front of it.

What height is the helicopter above the ground?

(It is not possible to give an actual scale drawing, but the method used is
explained below. You should try to make the drawing yourself.)

1. A suitable scale could be 1cm to 5 m.
   State this scale clearly.

2. First draw line AB of length 9.0 cm.

3. At A, measure an angle of 55°.

4. At B, <u>measure</u> an angle of 90°
   (do <u>not</u> just estimate a right angle!).

5. Continue the lines from A and from B
   to find the intersection point C.

6. Measure BC in the diagram (it should
   be approximately 12.9 cm).

7. Convert this into the real equivalent.

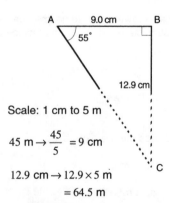

Scale: 1 cm to 5 m

$$45 \text{ m} \rightarrow \frac{45}{5} = 9 \text{ cm}$$

$$12.9 \text{ cm} \rightarrow 12.9 \times 5 \text{ m}$$
$$= 64.5 \text{ m}$$

The helicopter is
64.5 m above the ground.

4.12 ENLARGEMENT AND SIMILARITY

4.12.1 Scale Factors, Enlargements and Reductions

AB is a line. If a line A´B´ is drawn so that A´B´ = k x AB and k > 1, we say that A´B´ is an **enlargement** of AB and k is the **scale factor** of the enlargement.

eg   A_____B   A´_____B´

            A´B´ = 3 x AB   ie the scale factor is 3

If 0 < k < 1, we say that A´B´ is a **reduction** of AB.

The line A´B´ is called the **image of AB under the enlargement (reduction)**.

$$scale\ factor = \frac{image}{original} = \frac{A'B'}{AB}$$

In an enlargement (reduction) of a shape, every line is enlarged (reduced) by the same scale factor.

eg

         original   enlargement   reduction
                                      scale factor 1.5   scale factor 0.5

The equivalent sides in the original and the enlargement, eg the two lengths, are called **pairs of corresponding sides**.

In an enlargement, the **corresponding sides are in proportion**, since for each pair, $\frac{image}{original}$ gives the same value (the scale factor).

The examples in this topic can be done either by a **"ratio" method**, or by a **"multiplier" method** using the scale factor. Both methods are shown.

In the ratio method, the corresponding lengths in the original and the image are compared, setting up a ratio statement, which is then solved as an equation.

For the multiplier method, you use one pair of corresponding sides to find the scale factor, and then use that to find the unknown.

Example: A photo is 15 cm long by 10 cm wide.
An enlargement is required to have a length of 45 cm.
What width will it have?

Ratio Method:

$$\frac{\text{new width}}{\text{old width}} = \frac{\text{new length}}{\text{old length}}$$

$$\frac{w}{10} = \frac{45}{15}$$

$$w = \frac{45 \times 10}{15}$$

$$= 30$$

Multiplier Method:

$$\text{scale factor} = \frac{\text{new length}}{\text{old length}}$$

$$= \frac{45}{15} = 3$$

new width $= 3 \times$ old width

$$= 3 \times 10 = 30$$

Its width will be **30 cm**.

4.12.2 Similarity - Vocabulary   Ⓖ

You say two shapes are **equiangular** if they have the same angles in the same order. Note that the <u>order</u> of the angles is important.

For example, a parallelogram and a trapezium could both have two angles of $120°$ and two angles of $60°$ but would not be equiangular.

Two shapes are said to be **congruent** if they have exactly the same shape and size, ie they are equiangular and have sides of the same length.

Two shapes are said to be **similar** if one is an enlargement of the other, ie they are equiangular and have corresponding sides in proportion.

4.12.3 Problems Using Similarity

For most shapes, it is necessary to check that <u>both</u> the similarity properties (equiangular and corresponding sides in proportion) hold before deciding they are similar.

<u>For triangles only</u>, if one property holds then so does the other.
     If 2 triangles are equiangular, they are similar;
     if 2 triangles have corresponding sides in proportion, they are similar.

Note: You should be able to recognise and use similar shapes.
     You will <u>not</u> have to prove formally that shapes are similar.

     Similarity is in the syllabus at both the **G** and the **C** levels.
     At the **G** level, examples will only involve right-angled triangles or rectangles.

As for enlargement, examples can be done by ratio or multiplier methods. Again examples are shown using both methods.

Example 1: A post 2.6 m high has a shadow of length 7.2 m.
             A flag pole has a shadow of length 12.5 m.
             What height is the flag pole?

G

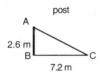

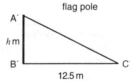

Since the angle of the sun is the same for both, the triangles are equiangular and therefore similar.

Ratio Method:

$$\frac{\text{height pole}}{\text{height post}} = \frac{\text{shadow pole}}{\text{shadow post}}$$

$$\frac{h}{2.6} = \frac{12.5}{7.2}$$

$$h = \frac{12.5}{7.2} \times 2.6$$

$$= 4.51...$$

Multiplier Method:

$$\text{scale factor} = \frac{\text{shadow pole}}{\text{shadow post}}$$

$$= \frac{12.5}{7.2} = 1.73...$$

$$\text{height of pole} = 1.73... \times \text{height of post}$$

$$= 1.73... \times 2.6$$

$$= 4.51...$$

The flag pole has height **4.5 m** to 1 dp.

It can be difficult to identify which sides are corresponding when using triangles.

It is helpful to remember that the longest sides in each will correspond.
Similarly, the shortest sides will correspond and the middle sides will correspond.

If there is not enough information about side lengths available, then note that the corresponding sides will always be opposite the equal angles in each triangle.

eg

Angles A and D are equal.
Therefore sides BC and EF are corresponding.

Example 2: A pair of stepladders has sizes as shown.
It has a horizontal support of length 90 cm, holding the front and back sections together. This is fastened 200 cm down from the top at the front.
How far apart would the sections be at the bottom?

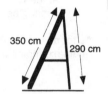

Make a drawing and introduce letters to help you explain what you are doing.

Since the horizontal support and the ground run parallel, △ABC and △ADE are equiangular and therefore similar. (Angles ABC and ADE, and ACB and AED are corresponding.)

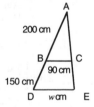

Ratio Method:

$$\frac{AB}{AD} = \frac{AC}{AE} = \frac{BC}{DE}$$
$$\frac{200}{350} = \frac{AC}{AE} = \frac{90}{w}$$
$$200w = 90 \times 350$$
$$w = \frac{90 \times 350}{200}$$
$$= 157.5$$

Multiplier Method:

$$\text{scale factor} = \frac{AD}{AB}$$
$$= \frac{350}{200} = 1.75$$
$$w = 1.75 \times BC$$
$$= 1.75 \times 90$$
$$= 157.5$$

The sections are **157.5 cm** apart at the bottom.

The following results on areas and volumes of similar shapes must be remembered.

Each of the results can be given in a ratio format or in a multiplier format. Both are given.

The multiplier format uses scale factors. The scale factor comparing the length of sides is referred to as the **linear scale factor**. The factor comparing areas is the **area scale factor**, and the factor comparing volumes is the **volume scale factor**.

4.12.4 Areas of Similar Shapes

For any pair of similar shapes:

Ratio Format

If the sides are in the ratio $a:b$, the areas are in the ratio $a^2:b^2$.

Multiplier Format

If the linear scale factor is k, the area scale factor is k^2.

Example: A box of chocolates has a triangular lid. The lid is 20 cm long along the longest side, and has an area of 250 cm^2.

A larger sized box of similar shape and length 30 cm can also be bought. What is the area of its lid?

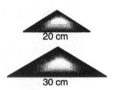

Ratio Method:

Ratio of sides $= 20:30$

$\qquad\qquad\quad = 2:3$

Ratio of areas $= 2^2:3^2$

$\qquad\qquad\quad = 4:9$

Ratios	Areas
4	→ 250
9	→ $\frac{9}{4} \times 250$
	$= 562.5$

Multiplier Method:

Linear scale factor $= \dfrac{\text{large}}{\text{small}}$

$\qquad\qquad = \dfrac{30}{20} = 1.5$

Area scale factor $= 1.5^2 = 2.25$

Area large $= 2.25 \times$ area small

$\qquad\quad = 2.25 \times 250$

$\qquad\quad = 562.5$

The large box has area **562.5 cm^2**.

Shape

4.12.5 Surface Areas and Volumes of Similar Solids

C/G

For any pair of similar solids:

Ratio Format

If the sides are in the ratio $a:b$, the areas are in the ratio $a^2:b^2$, the volumes are in the ratio $a^3:b^3$.

Multiplier Format

If the linear scale factor is k, the area scale factor is k^2, and the volume scale factor is k^3.

Note: Areas are **surface areas** - either the total area or individual sides.

Example 1: A bottle contains 150 ml. A similar shaped bottle is made which is 3 times as high. What is its volume?

Ratio Method:

Ratio of sides $= 1:3$

Ratio of volumes $= 1^3 : 3^3$

$\qquad = 1:27$

Ratios	Volumes
1	→ 150
27	→ $\dfrac{27}{1} \times 150$
	$= 4050$

Multiplier Method:

Linear scale factor $= 3$

Volume scale factor $= 3^3 = 27$

Volume large $= 27 \times$ volume small

$\qquad = 27 \times 150$

$\qquad = 4050$

The large bottle contains **4050 ml**.

Example 2: In the above example, if the small bottle is 12 cm high, what height is a bottle of twice the volume?

Ratio Method:

Ratio of volumes $= 1:2$

Ratio of heights $= \sqrt[3]{1}:\sqrt[3]{2}$

$\qquad = 1:\sqrt[3]{2}$

Ratios	Heights
1	→ 12
$\sqrt[3]{2}$	→ $\dfrac{\sqrt[3]{2}}{1} \times 12$
	$= 15.11...$

Multiplier Method:

Volume scale factor $= 2$

Linear scale factor $= \sqrt[3]{2}$

Height large $= \sqrt[3]{2} \times$ height small

$\qquad = \sqrt[3]{2} \times 12$

$\qquad = 15.11...$

The large bottle is **15.1 cm** high to 1dp.

5. TRIGONOMETRY

Trigonometry literally means the "measure of triangles".
Trigonometry looks at the relationships between angles and sides, firstly in the right angled triangle, and then in other triangles.

However, trigonometry goes beyond triangles to include the relationships between an angle and a number value produced by a trigonometric function.

5.1 THE RIGHT ANGLED TRIANGLE

5.1.1 Naming the Sides

The longest side (opposite the right angle) is called the **hypotenuse** (hyp).

In trigonometry, you are always interested in a particular angle.

The angle, if it is unknown, may be represented by a letter, eg x.

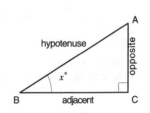

You may prefer to use a Greek letter like "theta" (θ) for angles.

The position of this angle determines the names of the other sides.
The side opposite the angle is called the **opposite** (opp),
and the side next to the angle is called the **adjacent** (adj).

5.1.2 The Trigonometric Ratios in the Right Angled Triangle

You can define 3 ratios in the right angled triangle which will always give the same values for a given angle $x°$, regardless of the size of triangle.

You call these ratios the **sine of** $x°$ (**sin** $x°$), the **cosine of** $x°$ (**cos** $x°$) and the **tangent of** $x°$ (**tan** $x°$). They are defined to be:

$$\sin x° = \frac{opp}{hyp} \qquad \cos x° = \frac{adj}{hyp} \qquad \tan x° = \frac{opp}{adj}$$

They must be remembered. You may find it helpful to use the first letter of each word:

SOH CAH TOA

It makes a nonsense word, but it seems to stick in most people's memory!

Trigonometry

5.1.3 Using a Calculator

To make use of the ratios, you must have another way of finding them. You can use a scientific calculator.

On some calculators, you enter the angle first and then the ratio. On others, you enter the ratio first. Check your own calculator.

eg $\quad\quad \sin 65.5°$ $\quad\quad$ Enter 65.5 then press **sin**,

$\quad\quad\quad\quad\quad$ or $\quad\quad$ press **sin** then enter 65.5.

$\quad\quad\quad$ Answer: 0.909 96...

Most trig questions will require rounding. 3 sf are usually sufficient for giving a trig ratio, and 1 dp for giving an angle, but it will depend on the question.
In practice, it is better to only round off the final answer (see Section 1.4).

When you know the sine value, for example, you must use the inverse sine to find the angle. You write this as:

$$\sin^{-1} x$$

On a calculator, this is usually obtained by pressing the **SHIFT** or **2nd Function** button then the **sin** button.

eg $\quad\quad \sin x° = 0.65$ $\quad\quad$ Enter 0.65 then press **shift** then **sin**,

$\quad\quad\quad\quad\quad$ or $\quad\quad$ press **shift** then **sin** then enter 0.65.

$\quad\quad\quad$ Answer: $x° = 40.541...°$

$\quad\quad$ **Note:** show the working as

$\quad\quad\quad \sin x° = 0.65$

$\quad\quad\quad x° = \sin^{-1} 0.65 = 40.541...°$

5.1.4 Using the Ratios - Finding an Angle

1. Use 2 of the sides to set up a ratio - sin, cos or tan.

2. Divide the numerator by the denominator to get a decimal value in the calculator.

3. Use the inverse trig ratio on the calculator to find the angle.

Example: In the diagram, what is the value of angle ABC, ie $x°$?

AB is the hyp, BC is the adj.
Therefore use the cos ratio.

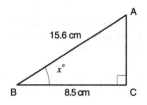

$$\cos x° = \frac{adj}{hyp} = \frac{8.5}{15.6} = 0.544...$$

$$x° = \cos^{-1} 0.544...$$

$$= 56.98...$$

Angle ABC is **57.0°** to 1dp.

5.1.5 Using the Ratios - Finding a Side 1 (numerator)

At the **G** level, the unknown side will always be in the numerator of the ratio.

1. Use 2 of the sides, including the unknown, to set up a ratio - sin, cos or tan - using the angle given.

2. Rearrange the equation to solve for the unknown.

3. Simplify.

Example: In the diagram, what is the length of AC, ie y cm?

AB is the hyp, AC is the opp.
Therefore use the sin ratio.

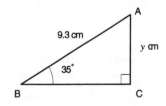

$$\sin 35° = \frac{opp}{hyp} = \frac{y}{9.3}$$

$$y = 9.3 \times \sin 35°$$

$$= 5.33...$$

Side AC is **5.3 cm** to 1dp.

Trigonometry

5.1.6 Using the Ratios - Finding a Side 2 (denominator)

At the **C/G** level, the unknown side can be in the denominator of the ratio. This leads to a more complicated rearrangement with the trig ratio ending up in the denominator.

1. Use 2 of the sides, including the unknown, to set up a ratio - sin, cos or tan - using the angle given.

2. Rearrange the equation to solve for the unknown.

3. Simplify.

Example: In the diagram, what is the length of BC, ie x cm?

AC is the opp, BC is the adj.
Use the tan ratio therefore.

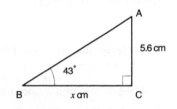

$$\tan 43° = \frac{opp}{adj} = \frac{5.6}{x}$$

$$x \tan 43° = 5.6$$

$$x = \frac{5.6}{\tan 43°}$$

$$= 6.00..$$

Side BC is **6.0 cm** to 1dp.

5.2 ANGLES OF ELEVATION AND DEPRESSION

The angle measured up from the horizontal to an object is called the **angle of elevation** of the object from that point.

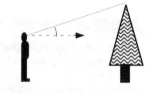

The angle measured down from the horizontal to an object is called the **angle of depression** of the object from that point.

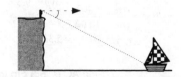

In small heights, it may be necessary to take the eye level of the person into account to get an accurate value. In larger measurements, it will not make a significant difference.

Revision Notes for

Example: The angle of elevation to the top of a hill, 10 km away, is 2.3°.
What height is the hill?

You must use the same kind of units for each side.
(10 km = 10 000 m)

$$\tan 2.3° = \frac{opp}{adj} = \frac{h}{10\ 000}$$

$$h = 10\ 000 \tan 2.3°$$

$$= 401.6...$$

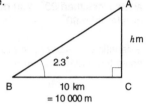

The hill is **402 m** high to the nearest metre.

5.3 GRADIENT OF A SLOPE Ⓖ

The gradient of a slope is defined to be

$$gradient = \frac{vertical\ \ height}{horizontal\ \ distance} = \frac{rise}{run}$$

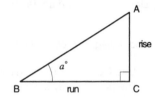

where the **rise** is the height gained vertically (AC), and the **run** is the distance gained horizontally (BC), in moving along the slope (BA).

If the slope goes **down**, the gradient will be **negative**.

If the slope makes an angle of $a°$ with the horizontal, the gradient will be tan $a°$.

Example: In the above example, a plane is taking off from the point of viewing.
At what gradient would it need to climb to be sure of clearing the hill?

$$h = 402\ m$$

$$(10\ km = 10\ 000\ m)$$

$$gradient = \frac{rise}{run} = \frac{402}{10\ 000}$$

$$= 0.040\ 2$$

or

$$gradient = \tan 2.3°$$

$$= 0.040\ 1...$$

$$= 0.040\ 2\ to\ 3\ sf$$

The plane would need to climb at a gradient of **greater than 0.04** (to 2 dp) to be
sure of clearing the hill.

5.4 ANGLES GREATER THAN 90°

The SOH CAH TOA ratios only work in right angled triangles, and therefore only for angles less than 90°. You need a new definition of sine, cosine and tangent for angles greater than 90°.

Scientific calculators are programmed to give values of the ratios beyond 90°, but to solve trig equations you must understand how this works.

5.4.1 Using Related Angles

You can find the sine, cosine or tangent of any angle $x°$ by relating it to an angle between 0° and 90°. This angle can be called the **related angle (RA)**.

The sine of angle $x°$ will be equal to either the positive or negative value of the sine of the related angle. The same applies to the cosine and the tangent.

The 3 diagrams below help to find the sine, cosine or tangent of any value.

1. Use Diagram 1 to decide which quadrant angle $x°$ is in.
   The positive x-axis is always taken as 0°, and angles are always measured anti clockwise from there. The full turn of 360° is then divided into 4 quadrants.

2. Use Diagram 2 to decide what the related angle is.
   The related angle is always the difference between the angle $x°$ and 0° / 180° / 360°. Never measure from 90° or 270°.

3. Use Diagram 3 to decide whether the ratio is positive or negative.
   The diagram tells which ratio(s) are positive in each quadrant.
   Think of the axes as a "positive sign" to help you remember.

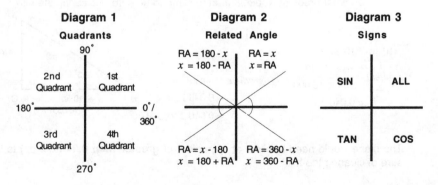

Example: Find (a) cos 163°,   (b) tan 225° in terms of their related angle, using the method above.

(a)
$$\cos 163°$$
2nd Quadrant
$$RA = 180 - 163$$
$$= 17°$$
cos is neg in 2nd Qu
$$\cos 163° = -\cos 17°$$
$$(= -0.956 \text{ to 3 dp})$$

(b)
$$\tan 225°$$
3rd Quadrant
$$RA = 225 - 180$$
$$= 45°$$
tan is pos in 3rd Qu
$$\tan 225° = \mathbf{tan45°}$$
$$(= 1)$$

In practice, if you only require the ratio value, you would find it directly using a calculator, but you will need this method for solving trig equations (see Section 5.6).

5.4.2 Alternative Method - Using the Trig Graphs

The same results can be obtained quite simply from the basic graph shapes (see Section 5.8).

The method is illustrated here using the sine graph.

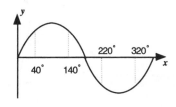

From the symmetry in the sine graph, you can see that there are 3 other values between 0° and 360° which have values related to sin 40°.

$$\sin 140° = \sin 40°$$
$$\sin 220° = -\sin 40°$$
$$\sin 320° = -\sin 40°$$

Notice that each angle is the same distance from either 0°, 180° or 360°.
In this example:

$$40° \ = \ 0° + 40° \qquad\qquad 140° \ = 180° - 40°$$
$$220° \ = 180° + 40° \qquad\qquad 320° \ = 360° - 40°$$

You can decide whether the ratio will be positive or negative by checking whether the graph is above or below the x axis.

The other ratios can be worked out in a similar way using their graphs.

5.5 THE TRIANGLE RULES

The following rules are for use with non-right angled triangles. They will work with right angled triangles as well, but they do not do anything that simple trigonometry will not do more easily.

It helps to make a sketch of the triangle to make sure you enter the correct sides and angles into the formula. It will also help you estimate your answer   (see Section 4.9 for naming sides).

5.5.1 The Sine Rule - Finding a Side

For any triangle ABC:

$$\frac{a}{\sin A} = \frac{b}{\sin B} = \frac{c}{\sin C}$$

You will normally get enough information to use two parts of the ratio.

Remember to use "the sum of angles in a triangle = 180°" to find extra information if required.

Example: In triangle ABC, angle A = 60°, angle B = 40° and BC = 6 cm. Find the length of AB.

Angle C = $180 - 40 - 60 = 80°$

By the Sine Rule,

$$\frac{a}{\sin A} = \frac{b}{\sin B} = \frac{c}{\sin C}$$

$$\frac{6}{\sin 60°} = \frac{b}{\sin 40°} = \frac{c}{\sin 80°}$$

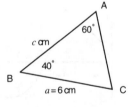

Use the first and last part to find c.

$$\frac{6}{\sin 60°} = \frac{c}{\sin 80°}$$

$$\frac{6\sin 80°}{\sin 60°} = c$$

$$c = 6.82...$$

Side AB is **6.8 cm** to 1 dp.

5.5.2 The Sine Rule - Finding an Angle

The above rule can be used in the same way to find an angle.

You may prefer to set it up with the sines in the numerator and the sides in the denominator in this case.

$$\frac{\sin A}{a} = \frac{\sin B}{b} = \frac{\sin C}{c}$$

It is important to remember that a positive sine value can give a 1st or 2nd Quadrant angle (see Section 5.6 on using the related angle (RA)).

This means you must always check whether a 2nd Quadrant angle would be a possible solution. The other angles will determine this.
If the 2nd Quadrant angle would result in the sum of angles being greater than 180°, then it is not a possible solution.

Example: In triangle ABC, side AC = 11.3 cm, side BC = 9.6 cm and angle
A = 45°. Find the possible sizes of angle B.

By the Sine Rule,

$$\frac{a}{\sin A} = \frac{b}{\sin B} = \frac{c}{\sin C}$$

$$\frac{9.6}{\sin 45°} = \frac{11.3}{\sin B} = \frac{c}{\sin C}$$

The two possible solutions are illustrated below.

Use the first two parts to find B.

$$\frac{9.6}{\sin 45°} = \frac{11.3}{\sin B}$$

$$9.6 \sin B = 11.3 \sin 45°$$

$$\sin B = \frac{11.3 \sin 45°}{9.6}$$

$$\sin B = 0.832...$$

$$RA = \sin^{-1} 0.832... = 56.33...$$

In the 1st Qu, $B = 56.33...$

In the 2nd Qu, $B = 180 - 56.33... = 123.66...$

which can also exist since $A + B = 168.7° < 180°$.

Angle B is **56.3°** or **123.7°** to 1 dp.

$\underline{B = 56.3°}$

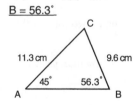

$\underline{B = 123.7°}$

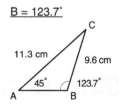

5.5.3 The Cosine Rule - Finding a Side

For any triangle ABC:

$$a^2 = b^2 + c^2 - 2bc \cos A$$

You must be able to give the formula with any side as the subject.

Example: In triangle ABC, angle A = 60°, AC = 4.2 cm and AB = 5.4 cm. Find the length of side BC.

By the Cosine Rule,

$$a^2 = b^2 + c^2 - 2bc \cos A$$
$$a^2 = 4.2^2 + 5.4^2 - 2 \times 4.2 \times 5.4 \times \cos 60°$$
$$= 24.12$$
$$a = \sqrt{24.12}$$
$$= 4.91...$$

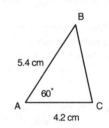

Side BC is **4.9 cm** to 1 dp.

5.5.4 The Cosine Rule - Finding an Angle

The above form of the Cosine Rule can be rearranged to find the size of an angle.

For any triangle ABC:

$$\cos A = \frac{b^2 + c^2 - a^2}{2bc}$$

You must be able to give the formula with the cosine of any angle as the subject.

Since the cosine of a 2nd Quadrant angle is negative, it will always be clear which quadrant the solution will be in.

Example: In triangle PQR, PQ = 12.5 cm, QR = 7.2 cm and PR = 8.1 cm.
Find the size of angle R.

By the Cosine Rule,

$$\cos R = \frac{p^2 + q^2 - r^2}{2pq}$$

$$\cos R = \frac{7.2^2 + 8.1^2 - 12.5^2}{2 \times 7.2 \times 8.1}$$

$$\cos R = \frac{-38.8}{116.64}$$

$$= -0.332...$$

$$R = \cos^{-1}(-0.332...) \quad \text{- 2nd Quadrant angle!}$$

$$= 109.42...$$

Angle R is **109.4°** to 1 dp.

5.5.5 The Area of a Triangle

C/G

For any triangle ABC, the area of the triangle is given by:

$$Area = \frac{1}{2}ab\sin C$$

You must be able to give the area using the sine of any of the angles (the example below requires the use of angle A).

Example: What is the area of the triangle ABC if AC = 6.5 cm, AB = 5.2 cm and angle A = 40°?

$$Area = \frac{1}{2}bc\sin A$$

$$= \frac{1}{2} \times 6.5 \times 5.2 \times \sin 40°$$

$$= 10.86...$$

The triangle has an area of **10.9 cm²** to 1 dp.

5.5.6 What Rule, When?

The following table summarises what information must be given to use each rule.

Rule	To Find...	Require to Know...
Sine Rule	side	an opposite angle and side and another angle
	angle	an opposite angle and side and another side
Cosine Rule	side	2 sides and the included angle
	angle	all 3 sides
Area of Triangle	Area	2 sides and the included angle

5.6 TRIGONOMETRIC EQUATIONS

5.6.1 Solving $\sin x° = k$ / $\cos x° = k$ / $\tan x° = k$ for $0 \leq x \leq 360$

Solving a trig equation of this type means finding all the possible angle values which have the required sine or cosine value.

The number of solutions will depend on what x, or angle, values are allowed in the question. There will usually be two values of x between 0° and 360°, producing the same sin or cos value.

A calculator can only give one answer, and in some cases, even that will not be an answer between 0° and 360°. You cannot rely on the calculator therefore.

You can make use of the same diagrams as those in Section 5.4.

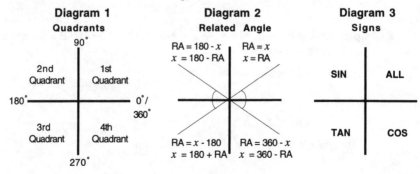

1. Use Diagram 3 to decide which quadrants the solutions, $x°$, will be in. There will always be 2 quadrants in which each ratio is either positive or negative.

2. Find the related angle (RA).
   Ignore any negative sign and find the angle between $0°$ and $90°$ which gives that ratio value. You can use the calculator for this.

3. Use Diagram 2 to decide what the solutions ($x°$ values) are.
   Remember, the related angle is always added to or subtracted from $0°$ / $180°$ / $360°$, never $90°$ or $270°$.
   Notice that in the 1st Quadrant, the related angle is the solution itself.

4. Use Diagram 1 to check that your solutions do lie in the correct quadrants.

5. Use your calculator to check that your solutions satisfy the equation.

Example 1: Solve $\sin x° = -0.5$ for $0 \le x \le 360$.

sine is negative in 3rd and 4th Quadrants

$$RA = \sin^{-1} 0.5 \text{ (Note: ignore the "−" sign.)}$$
$$= 30°$$

3rd Quadrant: $x° = 180 + RA$
$$= 180 + 30 = 210°$$

4th Quadrant: $x° = 360 - RA$
$$= 360 - 30 = 330°$$

Solution: $x° = \mathbf{210°}$ or $x° = \mathbf{330°}$

Alternative Method (using the trig graphs):

See Section 5.4.2 for further details of this method.

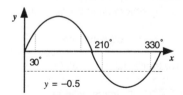

From the calculator, we find

$$\sin^{-1} 0.5 = 30°$$

From the graph, we see that
$$\sin x° = -0.5$$
in the 3rd and 4th quadrants.

So $x° = 180 + 30 = \mathbf{210°}$
and $x° = 360 - 30 = \mathbf{330°}$.

Example 2: Solve $\cos x° = 0.65$ for $0 \le x \le 360$.

cosine is positive in 1st and 4th Quadrants

$$RA = \cos^{-1} 0.65$$
$$= 49.45...$$

1st Quadrant : $x° = RA$
$$= 49.45... = 49.5° \text{ to 1 dp.}$$

4th Quadrant : $x° = 360 - RA$
$$= 360 - 49.45... = 310.5° \text{ to 1 dp.}$$

Solution : $\qquad x° = \mathbf{49.5°} \qquad$ or $\qquad x° = \mathbf{310.5°}$

Example 3: Solve $\tan x° = -2.5$ for $0 \le x \le 360$.

tangent is negative in 2nd and 4th Quadrants

$$RA = \tan^{-1} 2.5$$
$$= 68.1...$$

2nd Quadrant : $x° = 180 - RA$
$$= 180 - 68.1... = 111.8° \text{ to 1 dp.}$$

4th Quadrant : $x° = 360 - RA$
$$= 360 - 68.1... = 291.8° \text{ to 1 dp.}$$

Solution : $\qquad x° = \mathbf{111.8°} \qquad$ or $\qquad x° = \mathbf{291.8°}$

5.6.2 Solving $\sin x° = k$ / $\cos x° = k$ / $\tan x° = k$ for $0 \le x \le 180$

The methods used are the same as in Section 5.6.1, but only x values between $0°$ and $180°$ inclusive are valid solutions, and any others must be discounted.

The solutions to the previous examples for $0 \le x \le 180$ would be:

Example 1:   No solutions.   (Neither solution is valid.)

Example 2: $x° = 49.5°$.   ($x° = 310.5°$ is not valid.)

Example 3: $x° = 111.8°$.   ($x° = 291.8°$ is not valid.)

(The working would be identical to the previous examples.)

5.6.3 Solving $a\,\sin x° + b = c$ / $a\,\cos x° + b = c$ / $a\,\tan x° + b = c$

Equations of this type must first be rearranged to produce an equation of the type in Section 5.6.1, and then solved by the methods given there.

Example 1: Solve $2\sin x° = 1$ for $0 \leq x \leq 360$.

$$2\sin x° = 1$$
$$\sin x° = \frac{1}{2} = 0.5$$

sine is positive in 1st and 2nd Quadrants

$$RA = \sin^{-1} 0.5$$
$$= 30°$$

1st Quadrant: $x° = RA$
$$= 30°$$

2nd Quadrant: $x° = 180 - RA$
$$= 180 - 30 = 150°$$

Solution: $x° = \mathbf{30°}$ or $x° = \mathbf{150°}$

Example 2: Solve $3\cos x° + 2 = 0$ for $0 \leq x \leq 180$.

$$3\cos x° + 2 = 0$$
$$3\cos x° = -2$$
$$\cos x° = -\frac{2}{3} = -0.666...$$

cosine is negative in 2nd and 3rd Quadrants
However a 3rd Quadrant solution is not valid since $0 \leq x \leq 180$.

$$RA = \cos^{-1} 0.666...$$
$$= 48.18...°$$

2nd Quadrant: $x° = 180 - RA$
$$= 180 - 48.18... = 131.8°\text{ to 1 dp}$$

Solution: $x° = \mathbf{131.8°}$

5.7 TRIGONOMETRIC RELATIONSHIPS

You should know the following relationships. Although they will not be examined formally at Standard Grade, they are very important in Higher maths.

$$\sin^2 x° + \cos^2 x° = 1$$

$$\tan x° = \frac{\sin x°}{\cos x°}$$

5.8 TRIGONOMETRIC FUNCTIONS AND GRAPHS

Since sine, cosine and tangent are defined for angles other than 0° to 90°, you can regard them as functions and you should know the graphs that they produce.

All trigonometric graphs are **periodic**, ie they repeat their basic pattern continuously along the length of the graph.

Each basic pattern is called a **cycle**, and the length of a cycle is called the **period** of the graph.

The sine and cosine graphs are wave-shaped. The height of the wave above the centre line is called the **amplitude** of the wave.

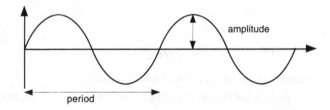

amplitude

period

5.8.1 The Basic Trigonometric Graphs

You must know the shapes of the three basic trig graphs - the sine graph, the cosine graph and, at the **C** level, the tangent graph.

The shape of the basic cycle is highlighted in bold.

You should know the significant features like period, amplitude and where each takes its maximum and minimum values.

The Sine Graph

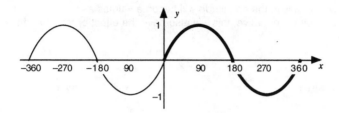

The Cosine Graph

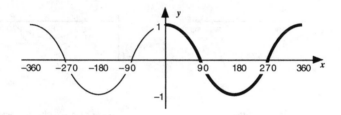

Both these graphs have an amplitude of 1, a maximum value of 1, a minimum value of −1, and a period of 360°.

The Tangent Graph

c

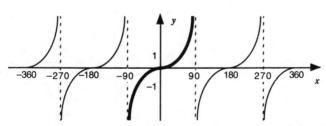

The tangent graph is not wave-shaped, but is periodic with a period of 180°.
There is no maximum or minimum value.
At 90° and 270° (and equivalent values), the tangent is not defined.

5.8.2 The Graph of $a \sin x°$ / $a \cos x°$

C

Multiplying $\sin x°$ or $\cos x°$ by a constant has the effect of stretching or squeezing the graph vertically about the x-axis.

If the constant is a, the amplitude will become a times as big.
If the constant is negative, this will also have the effect of reflecting the graph in the x-axis.

eg

$y = 2 \sin x°$

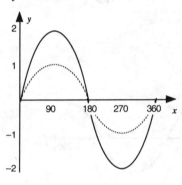

($y = \sin x°$ shown dotted)

$y = 0.5 \cos x°$

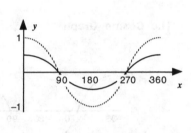

($y = \cos x°$ shown dotted)

$y = -2 \sin x°$

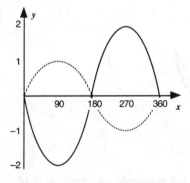

($y = \sin x°$ shown dotted)

$y = -0.5 \cos x°$

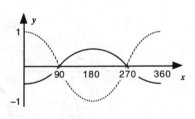

($y = \cos x°$ shown dotted)

C

5.8.3 The Graph of   sin $bx°$ / cos $bx°$

Multiplying x by a constant has the effect of stretching or squeezing the graph horizontally along the x-axis.

If the constant is b, there will be b complete cycles of the graph shown between 0° and 360°.

eg

$y = \sin 2x°$

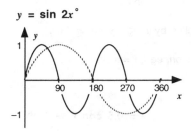

($y = \sin x°$ shown dotted)

$y = \cos 0.5x°$

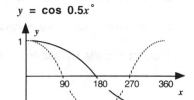

($y = \cos x°$ shown dotted)

C

5.8.4 The Graph of   sin $x° + c$ / cos $x° + c$

Adding or subtracting a constant c has the effect of shifting the graph up or down vertically by an amount c.

eg

$y = \sin x° + 2$

($y = \sin x°$ shown dotted)

$y = \cos x° - 0.5$

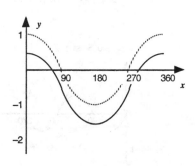

($y = \cos x°$ shown dotted)

5.8.5 The Graph of $a \sin bx° + c$ / $a \cos bx° + c$

The 3 transformations of the basic sine or cosine graph shown over may have to be combined to find an overall effect.

To find the resultant graph:

1. Sketch the basic sine or cosine graph, eg $y = \sin x°$.

2. Sketch the effect of multiplying $x°$ by b, eg $y = \sin bx°$.

3. Sketch the effect of multiplying this function by a, eg $y = a \sin bx°$.

4. Sketch the effect of adding c to this function, eg $y = a \sin bx° + c$.

eg

$y = \sin 2x° + 2$

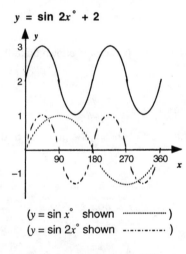

$y = 0.5 \cos x° - 1$

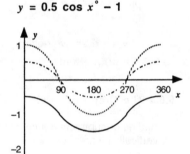

($y = \sin x°$ shown ··················)
($y = \sin 2x°$ shown ·-·-·-·-·-·)

($y = \cos x°$ shown ··················)
($y = 0.5 \cos x°$ shown ·-·-·-·-·)

$y = -0.5 \sin 2x°$

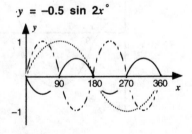

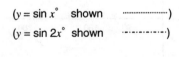

($y = \sin x°$ shown ··················)
($y = \sin 2x°$ shown ·-·-·-·-·)

5.9 BEARINGS

5.9.1 Three Figure Bearings

Bearings are measured in degrees from 0° to 360°, and normally written using 3 digits or figures. They are known as **3 figure bearings**.

They are measured **from north** (000°), **clockwise**.
When drawing a bearing, always take north **up the page**.

eg 135°   005°   270°

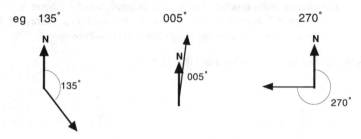

5.9.2 Plotting Points Given the Bearing
and Distance from Another Point

1. Mark a starting point, and draw the north arrow from that point.

2. Measure the bearing, draw the direction line and measure along the line to find the next point.

3. Draw another north arrow at that point and measure from there.

Example: A ship sails from A to B, a distance of 15 km on a bearing of 120°.
It then sails from B to C, a distance of 10 km on a bearing of 280°.
Draw the journey.
(This could lead into a scale drawing question.)

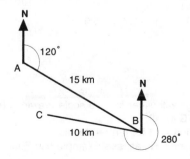

5.9.3 Plotting a Point Given the Bearings from 2 Points

1. Draw the north arrow from the two given points.

2. Measure the bearings and draw the direction lines from each point.

3. The required point will be at the intersection of the two direction lines.

Example: A radar station B is 50 km due east of another radar station A.
A plane at C is on a bearing of 075° from A and on a bearing of 300°
from B. Show the position of the plane on a scale drawing.

(A sketch is given here to illustrate the answer.)

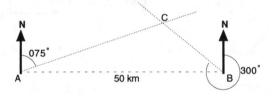

5.9.4 Calculating a Back Bearing

If the bearing from A to B is $a°$, then the bearing from B to A is called the **back bearing** of $a°$.

The back bearing of $a°$ will always be given by $(a \pm 180)°$. You choose to add or subtract depending on which will give an answer between 0° and 360°.

eg   If the bearing from A to B is 012°,
the bearing from B to A is 012 + 180 = 192°.

If the bearing from A to B is 279°,
the bearing from B to A is 279 − 180 = 099°.

5.9.5 Using Bearings

Most questions using bearings will either involve scale drawings (**G** level) or make use of the Triangle Rules (**C/G** level).
For scale drawings, see Section 4.11 for further details.
For an example using the Triangle Rules, see Example 6 in Section 8.2.3
(Modelling with Trigonometry).

6. RELATIONSHIPS

6.1 BASIC ALGEBRA

Algebra uses letters to represent numbers in two main ways:
- as a **variable** which can then take whatever value you choose to give it;
- as an **unknown** which can only take certain values depending on the information given.

Since letters must act like numbers, all the normal number rules must apply with letters as well.

6.1.1 Terms and Expressions

The basic components of algebra are called **terms**. They can contain both numbers and letters,

eg $\quad x, \quad 5x, \quad 2x^2, \quad -x^2, \quad 3y, \quad 2xy \quad$ are all terms.

You do not usually show a multiplication sign in algebra. When a letter and a number, or two letters, are written next to each other, this means they are multiplied together,

eg $\qquad 2x = 2 \times x \qquad xy = x \times y$.

Be careful not to confuse the following:

$$2x = 2 \times x = x + x \qquad x^2 = x \times x.$$

The type of term is determined by the letters contained in it. Terms which contain exactly the same letters are said to be **like terms**,

eg $\quad x$ and $5x$ are like terms, and are called x terms.

The order of the letters does not matter,

eg $\quad 2yx$ is the same as $2xy$.

The number in a term is called the **coefficient** of the term. You always write the number first,

eg -3 is the coefficient of $-3x^2y$.

Note: x means $1 \times x$. You do not normally show a 1 as a coefficient.

A number with no letter is called a **constant term**.

A sum or difference of terms is called an **expression**.

If the expression contains like terms, add or subtract these to **simplify the expression**. Always simplify an expression as much as possible.

eg $3x + 5x$ means 3 lots of x add on another 5 lots of x, so $3x + 5x = 8x$.

Note: $3x - x = 3x - 1x = 2x$. Do <u>not</u> just take the x off the $3x$ term to get 3.

Example: Simplify $3x^2 + 2xy + x - x^2 + 5xy - 6x$.

Note that there are 3 different types of terms.

These are x^2 terms, xy terms and x terms.

$$3x^2 + 2xy + x - x^2 + 5xy - 6x$$
$$= 3x^2 - x^2 + 2xy + 5xy + x - 6x$$
$$= 2x^2 + 7xy - 5x$$

Terms can be multiplied by numbers or by other terms.
Multiply the numbers together and the letters together.

eg $3 \times 2x = 6x$ $\qquad 3x \times 2x = 3 \times 2 \times x \times x = 6x^2$
$\quad 3x \times (-2y) = 3 \times (-2) \times x \times y = -6xy$

It is not normal to use the division sign '÷' in algebra.
Instead, division is normally written in the 'fraction form',

eg $\quad \dfrac{x}{2}$ means "x divided by 2".

The division of algebraic expressions is treated separately in Section 6.4.

6.1.2 Evaluating an Expression

When the overall value of an expression is found using particular values for the letters, you are **evaluating the expression** for the given values.

It is wise to put brackets round any negative value, as shown below, to help evaluate the expression correctly.

Example: When $x = 3$, $y = -2$ and $z = -5$, evaluate:

(a) $\quad x^2 + y^2 - z^2$
$$= 3^2 + (-2)^2 - (-5)^2$$
$$= 9 + 4 - 25$$
$$= -12$$

(b) $\quad 3xy + \dfrac{3z}{x-y}$
$$= 3 \times 3 \times (-2) + \dfrac{3 \times (-5)}{3 - (-2)}$$
$$= -18 + \dfrac{-15}{5}$$
$$= -18 + (-3)$$
$$= -21$$

6.2 MULTIPLYING BRACKETS

6.2.1 Multiplying Expressions 1 - a Bracket by a Number

When a number or letter appears immediately outside a bracket, you must multiply what is in the bracket by the number or the letter.

The **BODMAS** rule (see Section 1.2) says evaluate the bracket first.

eg $\quad 3(5 + 7) = 3 \times 12 = 36$

The same result as above can be obtained by multiplying <u>each</u> term in the bracket by the term outside.

eg $\quad 3(5 + 7) = 3 \times 5 + 3 \times 7 = 15 + 21 = 36$

You use this approach with algebraic expressions.

Example 1:

$2(x + 3)$
$= 2 \times x + 2 \times 3$
$= 2x + 6$

Example 2:

$4(x - 3)$
$= 4 \times x - 4 \times 3$
$= 4x - 12$

Example 3:

$5(2x + y)$
$= 5 \times 2x + 5 \times y$
$= 10x + 5y$

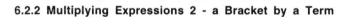

6.2.2 Multiplying Expressions 2 - a Bracket by a Term

At the **C/G** level, you may have to multiply through by an algebraic term.

A negative sign outside a bracket means multiply by -1.

Example 1:

$x(x + 3)$
$= x \times x + x \times 3$
$= x^2 + 3x$

Example 2:

$-(x - 3)$
$= -1 \times x - (-1) \times 3$
$= -x + 3$
$= 3 - x$

Example 3:

$3x(2x - 6y)$
$= 3x \times 2x - 3x \times 6y$
$= 3 \times 2 \times x \times x - 3 \times 6 \times x \times y$
$= 6x^2 - 18xy$

Example 4:

$$2x(x+3) - 3x(x-5)$$
$$= 2x \times x + 2x \times 3 - 3x \times x - 3x \times (-5)$$ **Note:** the 2 negative signs
$$= 2x^2 + 6x - 3x^2 + 15x$$ combine to give a positive.
$$= -x^2 + 21x$$
$$= 21x - x^2$$

6.2.3 Multiplying Expressions 3 - a Bracket by a Bracket   C/G C

You can multiply a bracket by a bracket by multiplying each term in the first bracket against each term in the second bracket.

The order of multiplying is not important, but you should follow the same procedures each time.

"first against first, first against second,
second against first, second against second"

$$(x+2)(x+3) = \ (x+2) \ (x+3)$$

$$= x \times x + x \times 3 + 2 \times x + 2 \times 3$$
$$= x^2 + 3x + 2x + 6$$
$$= x^2 + 5x + 6$$

Example 1:

$$(x+3)(2x-5)$$
$$= 2x^2 - 5x + 6x - 15$$
$$= 2x^2 + x - 15$$

Example 2:

$$(4x-3)(3x-7)$$
$$= 12x^2 - 28x - 9x + 21$$
$$= 12x^2 - 37x + 21$$

Example 3:

$$(x-y)(3x+2y)$$
$$= 3x^2 + 2xy - 3xy - 2y^2$$
$$= 3x^2 - xy - 2y^2$$

Harder examples involving, for example, brackets with more than 2 terms, are regarded as being at the **C** level.

Example 4:

$(x+2)(x^2-5x+3)$

$=x^3-5x^2+3x+2x^2-10x+6$

$=x^3-3x^2-7x+6$

Example 5:

$(x^2+2x)(x^3-3x^2)$

$=x^5-3x^4+2x^4-6x^3$

$=x^5-x^4-6x^3$

6.2.4 The Square of a Bracket

A bracket squared can be expanded either by multiplying the bracket by itself, as in Example 1 below, or by following the pattern given below.

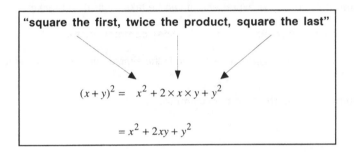

"square the first, twice the product, square the last"

$(x+y)^2 = x^2+2\times x\times y+y^2$

$= x^2+2xy+y^2$

Example 1:

$(x-y)^2$

$=(x-y)(x-y)$

$=x^2-xy-yx+y^2$

$=x^2-2xy+y^2$

Alternative Method:

$(x-y)^2$

$=x^2-2\times x\times y+y^2$

$=x^2-2xy+y^2$

Example 2:

$(2x+3)^2$

$=(2x+3)(2x+3)$

$=4x^2+6x+6x+9$

$=4x^2+12x+9$

Alternative Method:

$(2x+3)^2$

$=(2x)^2+2\times 2x\times 3+3^2$

$=4x^2+12x+9$

6.3 FACTORISING

A **factor** is a number which divides into a given number exactly,
  eg $12 = 1 \times 12 = 2 \times 6 = 3 \times 4$, so 1, 2, 3, 4, 6 and 12 are factors of 12.

The process of splitting into factors is called **factorisation**.

Algebraic expressions can sometimes be **factorised** into a product of simpler
expressions. Factorisation is the reverse process to multiplying out brackets.

There are 3 main types of algebraic factorisation.

6.3.1 Common Factor

If there is a term which is a factor of every term in an expression, you call it a
common factor of the expression. It can be taken outside a bracket.

To factorise fully, we must find the **highest common factor**.

At the **G** level, the only factor dealt with is the simple number common factor, as in
Example 1.

Example 1: Simple Number Common Factor

$$2x + 8 = 2 \times x + 2 \times 4$$
$$= 2(x + 4)$$

At the **C/G** level, the factor can be an algebraic term.

Example 2:   **Example 3:**

$x^2 - 5x$ $6x^2 + 15xy$
$= x \times x - 5 \times x$ $= 2 \times 3 \times x \times x + 3 \times 5 \times x \times y$
$= x(x - 5)$ $= 3x(2x + 5y)$

6.3.2 A Difference of 2 Squares

When 2 brackets which differ only in the signs, are multiplied together, you always
get 2 terms 'cancelling each other out'. The remaining terms are the squares of the
terms in the brackets.

eg $(x-y)(x+y) = x^2 + xy - yx - y^2$
$$= x^2 - y^2$$

This gives a standard pattern for factorising any expression which is 'a difference of 2 squares', ie one squared term minus another squared term.

$$\boxed{x^2 - y^2 = (x-y)(x+y)}$$

Example 1:

$x^2 - 25$
$= x^2 - 5^2$
$= (x-5)(x+5)$

Example 2:

$a^2 - b^2$
$= (a-b)(a+b)$

More complicated examples are regarded as being at the **C** level.

Example 3:

$9x^2 - 16y^2$
$= (3x)^2 - (4y)^2$
$= (3x-4y)(3x+4y)$

Example 4:

$x^4 - 9$
$= (x^2)^2 - (3)^2$
$= (x^2 - 3)(x^2 + 3)$

C

6.3.3 Two Brackets $(x^2 + bx + c)$

Any expression of the form
$$ax^2 + bx + c \quad (a \neq 0)$$
is called a **quadratic expression** (also referred to as a **trinomial**).

You can see some patterns when 2 brackets are multiplied together.

$(x+2)(x+5) = x^2 + 5x + 2x + 10 = x^2 + 7x + 10$
$(x+2)(x-5) = x^2 - 5x + 2x - 10 = x^2 - 3x - 10$
$(x-2)(x+5) = x^2 + 5x - 2x - 10 = x^2 + 3x - 10$
$(x-2)(x-5) = x^2 - 5x - 2x + 10 = x^2 - 7x + 10$

These lead to the following 'clues' for factorising a quadratic expression.

---

1. The x terms in the bracket are factors of the x^2 term.

2. The constant terms in the brackets are factors of the constant term.

3. The signs in the brackets are the same/different if the sign on the constant term is positive/negative.

4. The constant term in each bracket multiplied by the x term in the other bracket, add to give the x term.

You can use these 'clues' to help factorise a quadratic expression. You will have to use 'trial and improvement' to find the correct pair of brackets.

For example, to factorise $x^2 - 4x - 12$:

- the factors of x^2 are x and x,
- the factors of 12 are 1,12 or 2,6 or 3,4,
- the sign on 12 is negative, so the signs will be different,
- you require a pair with different signs to add to $-4x$, ie $-6x$ and $2x$.

Hence $x^2 - 4x - 12 = (x-6)(x+2)$.

You should always check your answer by multiplying the brackets out to see if you get the original expression.

Example 1:

$x^2 + 7x + 12$
$= (x+3)(x+4)$

Example 2:

$x^2 - 7x + 12$
$= (x-3)(x-4)$

Example 3:

$x^2 - 4x - 12$
$= (x-6)(x+2)$

6.3.4 Two Brackets $(ax^2 + bx + c)$

C

When the x^2 term has a coefficient other than 1, the quadratic is factorised in the same way as above, but the coefficient of the x^2 term must be factorised as well.

The x term will still be a combination of the x and constant terms in the brackets.

It is possible that instead of a quadratic in x, you may have a quadratic in x^2 (see Example 3 on the next page).

For example, to factorise $3x^2 + 10x + 8$:

 - the factors of $3x^2$ are $3x$ and x,
 - the factors of 8 are 1,8 or 2,4,
 - the sign on 8 is positive, so the signs will be the same,
 - you require a pair that combine with the same signs to give $+10x$,
  ie $3x \times 2 = 6x$ and $x \times 4 = 4x$.
 Hence $3x^2 + 10x + 8 \ = \ (3x + 4)(x + 2)$.

Example 1:

$2x^2 - 7x - 15$
$= (2x + 3)(x - 5)$

Example 2:

$6x^2 - 17x + 12$
$= (2x - 3)(3x - 4)$

Example 3:

$3x^4 - x^2 - 4$
$= (3x^2 - 4)(x^2 + 1)$

6.3.5 Mixed Factorising

C

When factorising, you should look for factors in the following order.

> **1. A Common Factor**
>
> **2. A Difference of 2 Squares**
>
> **3. A Pair of Brackets**

Watch for more than one type of factor being present, eg a common factor then a difference of squares, or a difference of squares twice.

An expression is not regarded as fully factorised until all possible factorisation has been completed.

Example 1:

$2x^3 - 18xy^2$
$= 2x(x^2 - 9y^2)$
$= 2x(x - 3y)(x + 3y)$

Example 2:

$x^4 - 1$
$= (x^2 - 1)(x^2 + 1)$
$= (x - 1)(x + 1)(x^2 + 1)$

Example 3:

$30x^2 - 75x - 45$
$= 15(2x^2 - 5x - 3)$
$= 15(2x + 1)(x - 3)$

6.4 ALGEBRAIC FRACTIONS

Almost all the work on algebraic fractions is at the **C** level.

Algebraic fractions follow the same rules as number fractions for simplifying and calculating (see Section 1.7).

6.4.1 Simplifying Algebraic Fractions

The basic rules for simplifying algebraic fractions are:

> **Factorise first.**
> **Only cancel factors.**

It is important to only cancel factors,

eg in $\dfrac{x+4}{4}$ you cannot cancel the 4's as the 4 in the numerator is not a factor.

Fractions at the **C/G** level will only involve simple terms, as in Examples 1 and 2.

Example 1:

$$\frac{6x^3}{2x} = \frac{\cancel{2} \times 3 \times \cancel{x} \times x^2}{\cancel{2} \times \cancel{x}}$$

$$= \frac{3x^2}{1} = 3x^2$$

Example 2:

$$\frac{8x^2}{6xy} = \frac{\cancel{2} \times 4 \times \cancel{x} \times x}{\cancel{2} \times 3 \times \cancel{x} \times y}$$

$$= \frac{4x}{3y}$$

Example 3:

$$\frac{(x+1)^2}{(x+1)^3} = \frac{\cancel{(x+1)}\cancel{(x+1)}}{(x+1)\cancel{(x+1)}\cancel{(x+1)}}$$

$$= \frac{1}{x+1}$$

Example 4:

$$\frac{x^2+2x+1}{x^2-1} = \frac{(x+1)\cancel{(x+1)}}{(x-1)\cancel{(x+1)}}$$

$$= \frac{x+1}{x-1}$$

C

6.4.2 Multiplying and Dividing Algebraic Fractions

1. Factorise first if necessary. Invert the second fraction in division.

2. Cancel any factors which are common to a numerator and denominator across any of the fractions.

3. Multiply the numerators together and the denominators together.

Some simple examples with number denominators could be at the **C/G** level.

Example 1:

$$\frac{x^2}{4} \times \frac{12}{x^3} = \frac{\cancel{x^2}^{\,1}}{\cancel{4}_1} \times \frac{\cancel{12}^{\,3}}{\cancel{x^3}_{\,x}}$$

$$= \frac{1}{1} \times \frac{3}{x}$$

$$= \frac{3}{x}$$

Example 2:

$$\frac{2xy}{9} \div \frac{8y}{6x} = \frac{2xy}{9} \times \frac{6x}{8y}$$

$$= \frac{\cancel{2xy}^{\,x}}{\cancel{9}_3} \times \frac{\cancel{6x}^{\,2x}}{\cancel{8y}_4}$$

$$= \frac{x}{3} \times \frac{\cancel{2x}^{\,x}}{\cancel{4}_2} = \frac{x^2}{6}$$

Example 3:

$$\frac{x^2 + x}{x} \times \frac{x^2}{x^2 - 1}$$

$$= \frac{x(x+1)}{x} \times \frac{x^2}{(x-1)(x+1)}$$

$$= \frac{\cancel{x}^{\,1}\cancel{(x+1)}^{\,1}}{\cancel{x}_1} \times \frac{x^2}{(x-1)\cancel{(x+1)}_1}$$

$$= \frac{x^2}{x-1}$$

Example 4:

$$\frac{x^2 + 4x + 3}{x^2 - 9} \div \frac{1}{x^2}$$

$$= \frac{(x+3)(x+1)}{(x-3)(x+3)} \times \frac{x^2}{1}$$

$$= \frac{\cancel{(x+3)}^{\,1}(x+1)}{(x-3)\cancel{(x+3)}_1} \times \frac{x^2}{1}$$

$$= \frac{x^2(x+1)}{x-3}$$

6.4.3 Adding and Subtracting Algebraic Fractions

1. Factorise first if necessary.

2. Find the lowest common denominator, and change all the fractions to this by multiplying the numerator and denominator by the same value.

3. Add or subtract the numerators, simplifying if necessary.

Some simple examples with number denominators, like Example 1, could be at the **C/G** level.

Example 1:

$$\frac{x}{2} + \frac{2x}{3}$$

$$= \frac{3x}{6} + \frac{4x}{6}$$

$$= \frac{7x}{6}$$

Example 2:

$$\frac{x+1}{x} - \frac{2}{3x^2}$$

$$= \frac{3x(x+1)}{3x^2} - \frac{2}{3x^2}$$

$$= \frac{3x^2 + 3x - 2}{3x^2}$$

Example 3:

$$\frac{1}{x-2} + \frac{2}{x+3}$$

$$= \frac{1(x+3)}{(x-2)(x+3)} + \frac{2(x-2)}{(x-2)(x+3)}$$

$$= \frac{x+3+2x-4}{(x-2)(x+3)}$$

$$= \frac{3x-1}{(x-2)(x+3)}$$

Example 4:

$$\frac{5}{x^2-1} - \frac{3}{x^2+x}$$

$$= \frac{5}{(x-1)(x+1)} - \frac{3}{x(x+1)}$$

$$= \frac{5x}{x(x-1)(x+1)} - \frac{3(x-1)}{x(x+1)(x-1)}$$

$$= \frac{5x - 3(x-1)}{x(x-1)(x+1)}$$

$$= \frac{5x - 3x + 3}{x(x-1)(x+1)}$$

$$= \frac{2x + 3}{x(x-1)(x+1)}$$

6.5 LINEAR EQUATIONS

With equations, you use the letter to represent the **unknown**.

When you **solve an equation**, you are finding the value(s) of the unknown that fits the equation. This is called the **solution of the equation**. The solution(s) can also be known as the **root(s)** of the equation.

An equation which contains only x terms and constant terms is called a **linear equation**,

eg $ax + b = cx + d.$

You can create an equivalent equation, ie another with the same solution, by:

> **adding (or subtracting) the same term to (from) each side of an equation,**
>
> **or**
>
> **multiplying (or dividing) each side of an equation by the same term.**

You can simplify an equation by using these results to 'get rid' of some of the terms.

eg

$$x + 5 = 15$$
$$[x + 5 - 5 = 15 - 5]$$
$$x = 15 - 5$$
$$x = 10$$

$$x - 2 = 6$$
$$[x - 2 + 2 = 6 + 2]$$
$$x = 6 + 2$$
$$x = 8$$

$$3x = 18$$
$$\left[\frac{3x}{3} = \frac{18}{3}\right]$$
$$x = \frac{18}{3}$$
$$x = 6$$

$$\frac{x}{5} = 4$$
$$\left[5 \times \frac{x}{5} = 5 \times 4\right]$$
$$x = 5 \times 4$$
$$x = 20$$

The bracketed step in each is often missed out. It looks as if the term in each case moves to the other side of the equation where it appears with the opposite sign.

As a result, some people choose to remember this by a rule like:

> **change side, change sign**
> or
> **change side, change operation**

Be careful if you use a rule like this. It is important that you understand why it works or you may end up changing signs when you should not.

6.5.1 Simple Linear Equations

1. Collect the x terms on the left and the constant terms on the right.

2. Simplify to solve for x.

Example 1:

$$3x + 2 = 17$$
$$3x = 17 - 2$$
$$3x = 15$$
$$x = 5$$

Example 2:

$$7x - 5 = 3x + 11$$
$$7x - 3x = 11 + 5$$
$$4x = 16$$
$$x = 4$$

6.5.2 Linear Equations - Harder Examples

C/G C

1. Remove any fractions first by multiplying through the equation by the lowest common multiple of the denominators.

   (It is possible to deal with fractions using the methods for algebraic fractions, as in Section 6.4, but it is much simpler to remove them this way.)

2. Multiply out any brackets.

3. Collect the x terms on the left and the constant terms on the right.

4. Simplify to solve for x.

Examples at this level may result in a negative x term at step 3. You may prefer to collect the x terms on the right to avoid this (see Example 1 below).

It is also possible to rewrite the equation, switching the left and right hand sides.

Example 1:

$$x + 3 = 5x - 13$$
$$x - 5x = -13 - 3$$
$$-4x = -16$$
$$4x = 16$$
$$x = 4$$

Alternative Method:

$$x + 3 = 5x - 13$$
$$3 + 13 = 5x - x$$
$$16 = 4x$$
$$4 = x$$
$$\text{or } x = 4$$

Example 2:

$$2x - 1 = 5x + 9$$
$$2x - 5x = 9 + 1$$
$$-3x = 10$$
$$x = \frac{10}{-3}$$
$$x = -3\frac{1}{3}$$

Example 3:

$$3x - 2(x - 5) = 4(3 - x)$$
$$3x - 2x + 10 = 12 - 4x$$
$$3x - 2x + 4x = 12 - 10$$
$$5x = 2$$
$$x = \frac{2}{5}$$

The harder fraction equations are at the **C** level.

C

Example 4:

$$\frac{x}{2} + \frac{x}{3} = \frac{1}{4}$$
Multiply each term by 12.
$$12 \times \frac{x}{2} + 12 \times \frac{x}{3} = 12 \times \frac{1}{4}$$
$$6x + 4x = 3$$
$$10x = 3$$
$$x = \frac{3}{10}$$

Example 5:

$$\frac{5(x - 1)}{3} - \frac{2(2x + 1)}{5} = 1$$
Multiply each term by 15.
$$15 \times \frac{5(x - 1)}{3} - 15 \times \frac{2(2x + 1)}{5} = 15 \times 1$$
$$25(x - 1) - 6(2x + 1) = 15$$
$$25x - 25 - 12x - 6 = 15$$
$$25x - 12x = 15 + 25 + 6$$
$$13x = 46$$
$$x = \frac{46}{13}$$
$$x = 3\frac{7}{13}$$

6.5.3 Literal Equations

C/G

A **literal equation** is an equation where letters are used as **variables** to represent numbers, as well as for the **unknown**.

They are solved in the same way as number equations, but the solution will be given in terms of the other letters.

Example 1:

$$ax + b = c$$
$$ax = c - b$$
$$x = \frac{c-b}{a}$$

Example 2:

$$T = \frac{bx^2}{a} - c$$
$$aT = bx^2 - ac$$
$$aT + ac = bx^2$$
$$bx^2 = aT + ac$$
$$x^2 = \frac{aT + ac}{b}$$
$$x = \sqrt{\frac{aT + ac}{b}}$$

Example 3:

$$a(x - b) = cx$$
$$ax - ab = cx$$
$$ax - cx = ab$$
$$x(a - c) = ab$$
$$x = \frac{ab}{a - c}$$

This example shows how to deal with more than one x term.

You must remember to make use of a 'common factor'.

6.6 QUADRATIC EQUATIONS

An equation containing x^2, x, and constant terms is called a **quadratic equation**. All quadratic equations can be written in the **standard form**:
$$ax^2 + bx + c = 0 \qquad (a \neq 0)$$

> To solve a quadratic equation, first try factorising.
>
> If the equation does not factorise, try the formula.

A quadratic equation will normally have two solutions or roots. Sometimes these will be the same, and you call them **equal roots**. It is possible that there will be no solutions at all.

If the equation can factorise, the solutions will be integer or rational. The formula will usually give irrational roots. These must be rounded or left as exact values using surds.

6.6.1 Solving by Factorising

You make use of factorising and the basic result:

" If $A \times B = 0$, then $A = 0$ or $B = 0$. "

1. Arrange the equation into the standard form with the right hand side equal to 0.

2. Factorise the quadratic expression on the left hand side.

3. This will result in simple linear equations which can be solved the usual way.

Example 1:

$$x^2 - 2x - 15 = 0$$
$$(x - 5)(x + 3) = 0$$
$$x - 5 = 0 \text{ or } x + 3 = 0$$
$$x = 5 \text{ or } x = -3$$

Example 2 (equal roots):

$$x^2 - 8x + 16 = 0$$
$$(x - 4)(x - 4) = 0$$
$$x - 4 = 0 \text{ or } x - 4 = 0$$

Both give the same solution,

$$x = 4$$

Some of the harder examples will be at the **C** level,
eg   factorising leading to non-integer solutions (Example 3),
       equations which do not look "quadratic" at first (Example 4).

Example 3:

$$2x^2 + x = 6$$
$$2x^2 + x - 6 = 0$$
$$(2x - 3)(x + 2) = 0$$
$$2x - 3 = 0 \text{ or } x + 2 = 0$$
$$2x = 3 \text{ or } x = -2$$
$$x = \tfrac{3}{2} \text{ or } x = -2$$

Example 4:

$$x - 1 = \frac{2}{x}$$

Multiply by x

$$x^2 - x = 2$$
$$x^2 - x - 2 = 0$$
$$(x - 2)(x + 1) = 0$$
$$(x - 2) = 0 \text{ or } (x + 1) = 0$$
$$x = 2 \text{ or } x = -1$$

6.6.2 Solving by Formula

If a quadratic equation cannot factorise, you can try to solve it by using the **quadratic formula**:

$$\text{If } ax^2 + bx + c = 0, \ (a \neq 0) \text{ then}$$

$$x = \frac{-b \pm \sqrt{b^2 - 4ac}}{2a}.$$

1. Arrange into the standard form with the right hand side equal to 0.

2. Substitute the values for a, b and c into the formula.

Extra care must be taken when any of the coefficients are negative.

Example 1:

$$2x^2 + 6x + 1 = 0$$
$$a = 2 \quad b = 6 \quad c = 1$$
$$x = \frac{-b \pm \sqrt{b^2 - 4ac}}{2a}$$
$$x = \frac{-6 \pm \sqrt{6^2 - 4 \times 2 \times 1}}{2 \times 2}$$
$$x = \frac{-6 \pm \sqrt{36 - 8}}{4}$$
$$x = \frac{-6 + \sqrt{28}}{4} \quad \text{or} \quad x = \frac{-6 - \sqrt{28}}{4}$$
$$x = -0.177... \quad \text{or} \quad x = -2.822...$$
$$x = \mathbf{-0.2} \quad \text{or} \quad x = \mathbf{-2.8} \quad \text{to 1 dp}$$

Example 2:

$$x^2 - 4 = 5x$$
$$x^2 - 5x - 4 = 0$$
$$a = 1 \quad b = -5 \quad c = -4$$
$$x = \frac{-b \pm \sqrt{b^2 - 4ac}}{2a}$$
$$x = \frac{-(-5) \pm \sqrt{(-5)^2 - 4 \times 1 \times (-4)}}{2 \times 1}$$
$$x = \frac{5 \pm \sqrt{25 + 16}}{2}$$
$$x = \frac{5 + \sqrt{41}}{2} \quad \text{or} \quad x = \frac{5 - \sqrt{41}}{2}$$
$$x = 5.701... \quad \text{or} \quad x = -0.701...$$
$$x = \mathbf{5.7} \quad \text{or} \quad x = \mathbf{-0.7} \quad \text{to 1 dp}$$

6.7 LINEAR INEQUATIONS

An **inequation** is a statement like an equation except it uses an inequality sign instead of an equals sign.

<	is less than	≤	is less than or equal to
>	is greater than	≥	is greater than or equal to

6.7.1 Simple Linear Inequations

The methods of solution are similar to those for equations.

Example 1:

$$3x + 2 \le 14$$
$$3x \le 14 - 2$$
$$3x \le 12$$
$$x \le 4$$

Example 2:

$$5x - 3 > 32$$
$$5x > 32 + 3$$
$$5x > 35$$
$$x > 7$$

6.7.2 Linear Inequations Involving Negatives

At the **C/G** level, you must be able to deal with negative x terms. This is the only case that requires a different treatment from equations.

You must remember to change the inequality sign when you change from negative to positive, ie $-2x < 4$ is equivalent to $2x > -4$.

Example 1:

$$4 - 2x > 10$$
$$-2x > 10 - 4$$
$$-2x > 6$$
$$2x < -6$$
$$x < -3$$

Example 2:

$$x - 6 \le 5x - 12$$
$$x - 5x \le -12 + 6$$
$$-4x \le -6$$
$$4x \ge 6$$
$$x \ge \frac{6}{4}$$
$$x \ge \frac{3}{2}$$

6.8 SIMULTANEOUS EQUATIONS

An equation containing x terms, y terms and number terms is called a **linear equation in two variables**,

eg $x + 2y = 4$.

An equation of this type will have an infinite number of solutions,

eg $x = 4$, $y = 0$;　$x = 2$, $y = 1$;　$x = 0$, $y = 2$;　etc.

When you try to find values which are solutions to 2 or more such equations at the same time, you are said to be **solving the equations simultaneously**.

6.8.1 Solving by Graph

The graphical method can be useful, but it is also time-consuming and does not result in accurate solutions. Do not use this method unless you are told to do so.

If you plot the solutions of a linear equation in 2 variables, you get a straight line (see Section 4.7).

You can use a graph therefore to solve a pair of equations.

1. Draw the line for each equation (see Section 4.7.2 for details of the method).

2. The intersection point of the lines will give the solution of the equations.

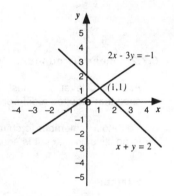

Example: Solve simultaneously $x + y = 2$ and $2x - 3y = -1$.

From the graph, the intersection point is $(1,1)$, so the solution is $x = 1, y = 1$.

6.8.2 Solving by Elimination

You can add two equations together to produce a third,
    eg adding $x + y = 3$ and $2x - 3y = 5$ gives $3x - 2y = 8$.

You can multiply an equation by a number to produce another equation,
    eg multiplying $x + y = 3$ by 3 gives $3x + 3y = 9$.

You can use these ideas to solve a pair of equations as follows.

1. Arrange both equations in the form $ax + by = c$.

2. Multiply each equation to get the coefficients of y (or you can choose x) to the <u>same number</u> but with <u>different signs</u>.

3. Add the equations - the y terms will cancel each other out and give an equation in x only.

4. Solve to find x and substitute this value into either equation to find y.

Example: Solve simultaneously $3x + 2y = 8$ and $2x + 5y = -2$.

$3x + 2y = 8$ **Equation 1** $\qquad\qquad$ $2x + 5y = -2$ **Equation 2**

(1) $\times 5$ $\quad 15x + 10y = 40$ $\qquad$ Substitute 4 for x in **(1)**
(2) $\times (-2)$ $-4x - 10y = 4$ $\qquad\qquad$ $3 \times 4 + 2y = 8$
Add $\qquad\quad 11x + 0 = 44$ $\qquad\qquad\qquad$ $2y = 8 - 12$
$\qquad\qquad\qquad 11x = 44$ $\qquad\qquad\qquad\qquad$ $2y = -4$
$\qquad\qquad\qquad\quad x = 4$ $\qquad\qquad\qquad\qquad$ $y = -2$

The solution is $x = 4$, $y = -2$.
(Check that your solution fits both the equations.)

6.8.3 Solving by Substitution

This method is particularly useful if one of the equations is non-linear.

1. Rearrange the linear equation into the form $y = \ldots$

2. Substitute this into the other equation in place of y.

3. Solve the resulting equation for x (often a quadratic resulting in more than 1 solution).

4. Substitute the x values into the <u>linear equation</u> to find the y values.

Example: Solve simultaneously $y = x^2$ and $y = x + 2$.

$y = x^2$ **Equation 1** $\qquad\qquad$ $y = x + 2$ **Equation 2**
$\qquad\quad y = x^2$
Substitute $x + 2$ for y in **(1)**
$\qquad\quad x + 2 = x^2$
$\qquad\qquad x^2 = x + 2$
$\quad x^2 - x - 2 = 0$ $\qquad\qquad$ Substitute 2 and -1 for x in **(2)**
$\quad (x - 2)(x + 1) = 0$ $\qquad\qquad$ $y = x + 2$ $\qquad\quad$ $y = x + 2$
$\quad x - 2 = 0$ or $x + 1 = 0$ $\qquad$ $y = 2 + 2$ $\qquad\quad$ $y = -1 + 2$
$\qquad x = 2$ or $x = -1$ $\qquad\qquad$ $y = 4$ $\qquad\qquad$ $y = 1$

The solutions are $x = 2$, $y = 4$ and $x = -1$, $y = 1$.

6.9 NUMERICAL (APPROXIMATE) SOLUTIONS OF EQUATIONS

Equations other than linear and quadratics are difficult to solve by algebraic methods. The following method can be used with any equation, but is particularly useful for equations other than linear or quadratic.

6.9.1 Finding an Approximate Solution

C

You must first obtain an approximation to the solution of the equation. This might be given in a question, but is often found using a graph, as in the example below.

Example: Use a graph to show that the equation $\dfrac{4}{x} = x+1$ has a root between $x = 1$ and $x = 2$, and estimate the root.

1. Draw the graph of each 'side' of the equation,

   ie $\quad y = \dfrac{4}{x}\quad$ and $\quad y = x+1$

   by plotting points or sketching (see Sections 6.12 and 4.7).

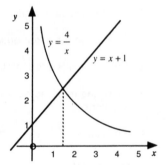

2. The intersection point of the lines will give a solution of the above equation.

   In this example,
   x is approximately 1.5.

Alternative Method:

It is also possible to rearrange the equation into the "... = 0" form,

   ie $\quad \dfrac{4}{x} - x - 1 = 0,$

and plot the graph of the left hand side. The solution will then be where the graph cuts the x axis.

This is the function you use to 'home in' on the root (see the following section), so it can be helpful to graph it here.

6.9.2 Improving the Solution by Iteration

C

Iteration is a repetitive process in which you input a value and use it to find a better value, which is then used to find another better value, and so on.

If a is a solution of the equation $f(x) = 0$, then $f(a) = 0$. The graph of $y = f(x)$ will cut the x axis at the root a (see Section 6.12 for function notation).

For x values on either side of a,
$f(x)$ will have a different sign, either
    positive for $x < a$ and negative for $x > a$,
or
    negative for $x < a$ and positive for $x > a$
(see diagram).

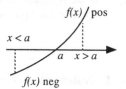

You can identify which x values lie on each side of the actual root by checking the sign of $f(x)$ for each x value.

By continuing to find values on either side of the root which are getting closer together, you can identify the root to the required accuracy.

Example (continued from Section 6.9.1):

Find the solution of the equation $\dfrac{4}{x} = x + 1$

correct to 2 decimal places, given 1.5 as a first approximation.

1. Rearrange the equation to give $f(x) = 0$.

2. Evaluate $f(x)$ for the initial approximation, noting whether the value obtained is positive or negative.

3. Repeat this for other values which 'sandwich' the actual root more closely, until the desired accuracy has been obtained. It is often helpful to halve the interval between the last 2 approximations. Record the values in a table.

$$\frac{4}{x} = x + 1$$

$$\frac{4}{x} - x - 1 = 0$$

Let $\quad f(x) = \dfrac{4}{x} - x - 1$

$f(1.5) = +0.16...$
$f(1.6) = -0.1$
$f(1.55) = +0.03...$
$f(1.57) = -0.02...$
$f(1.56) = +0.004...$
$f(1.565) = -0.009...$

x values $f(x)$ pos	x values $f(x)$ neg
1.5	1.6
1.55	1.57
1.56	1.565

So the actual root lies between 1.56 and 1.565, ie the root is **1.56** to 2 dp.

6.10 FORMULAE

A **formula** is a mathematical rule. It will normally be expressed using numbers and symbols as variables,

eg $\quad M = \frac{5}{8}K, \qquad S = \frac{D}{T}, \qquad v = u + at, \qquad s = \frac{v^2 - u^2}{2a}.$

A formula will normally have a **subject** (M, S, v and s in the above examples), an equals sign and an algebraic expression.

6.10.1 Evaluating a Formula

G

Replace each letter by the given value and calculate (see Section 6.1.2).

Example: If $s = \frac{v^2 - u^2}{2a}$, find the value of s when $u = 4$, $v = 6$ and $a = 3$.

$$s = \frac{6^2 - 4^2}{2 \times 3} = \frac{36 - 16}{6} = \frac{20}{6} = 3\frac{1}{3}$$

6.10.2 Changing the Subject of a Formula

C/G

Changing the subject of a formula means rearranging the formula to make a different letter the subject. Use the same methods as in Section 6.5.3 (Literal Equations).

Example: Make v the subject of the equation $s = \frac{v^2 - u^2}{2a}$.

$$s = \frac{v^2 - u^2}{2a}$$
$$2as = v^2 - u^2$$
$$v^2 - u^2 = 2as$$
$$v^2 = u^2 + 2as$$
$$v = \sqrt{u^2 + 2as}$$

6.10.3 The Effect of a Change in a Variable

Given certain changes in the variable(s) of a formula, you have to determine the overall effect on the subject of the formula.

1. For each variable, substitute an expression showing the change in the variable, eg if a has doubled, substitute in $2a$.

2. Rearrange the formula expression to get a multiple of the original formula expression. The multiple then gives the effect on the subject.

Example 1: If $P = 200\dfrac{T}{V}$, what is the effect on P of doubling T and halving V?

$$T \rightarrow 2T \qquad V \rightarrow 0.5V \qquad P \rightarrow P'$$

$$P' = 200\frac{2T}{0.5V}$$

$$P' = \frac{2}{0.5}\left(200\frac{T}{V}\right)$$

$$P' = 4P \qquad P \text{ becomes } \textbf{4 times as big.}$$

In some examples, the increase / decrease is given as a percentage.

Remember that a 20% increase is equivalent to producing 120%, ie 'x 1.2', and a 20% decrease is equivalent to producing 80%, ie 'x 0.8'.

Example 2: If $T = 2\dfrac{x^2}{\sqrt{y}}$, what is the effect on T of a 20% increase in x

and a 10% decrease in y?

$$x \rightarrow 1.2x \qquad y \rightarrow 0.9y \qquad T \rightarrow T'$$

$$T' = 2\frac{(1.2x)^2}{\sqrt{0.9y}}$$

$$T' = 2\frac{1.2^2 x^2}{\sqrt{0.9}\sqrt{y}}$$

$$T' = \frac{1.2^2}{\sqrt{0.9}} \times \left(2\frac{x^2}{\sqrt{y}}\right)$$

$$T' = 1.517... \times T \qquad\qquad T \text{ becomes } \textbf{52\% bigger.}$$

6.10.4 Number Patterns Ⓖ

You need to be able to both extend a sequence of numbers and to give a formula for finding a term in the sequence. It is helpful to talk about the nth **term** in the sequence, and to give a **formula for the nth term** in terms of n.

You should be familiar with the following common sequences:

Types of Numbers	Examples	Formula for nth term
Even numbers	2, 4, 6, 8, 10, ...	$2n$
Odd numbers	1, 3, 5, 7, 9, ...	$2n-1$
Square numbers	1, 4, 9, 16, 25, ...	n^2
Triangular numbers	1, 3, 6, 10, 15, ...	$\dfrac{n(n+1)}{2}$
Cube numbers	1, 8, 27, 64, 125, ...	n^3

6.10.5 Finding a Formula for Number Patterns Ⓖ

You must be able to find a formula, either for a sequence of numbers, or from a table of values.

The following hints should help:

1. If the numbers go up by a constant value k each time, try a '$x\ k$' in the formula.

Example 1: Find a formula for y in terms of x, for the values in the table.

x	1	2	3	4	5
y	4	7	10	13	16

The y values go up by 3 each time, so try $y = 3x + a$.

By checking, a must be 1
so $y = 3x + 1$.

2. If the numbers go up by an increasing amount each time, check for square or triangular numbers or a product of terms.

Example 2: Find the next 2 terms and a formula for the nth term in the sequence   4, 10, 18, 28, ...

4   10   18   28   **40**   **54**   The next 2 terms are **40** and **54**.
 +6   +8   +10   +12   +14

To find the formula, you must experiment with number patterns. It helps to set out a table, comparing the sequence values with the n values, n^2 values, etc.

sequ	4	10	18	28	40	54
n	1	2	3	4	5	6
n x n	1	4	9	16	25	36
sequ	1+3	4+6	9+9	16+12	25+15	36+18
n x n + 3 x n	4	10	18	28	40	54

The formula for the nth term is $n^2 + 3n$.

3. It often helps to consider how a pattern is created when considering a pattern arising in a context.

Example 3: How many lengths of wire will there be when there are n posts?

2 posts	1 set of 2 wires + the end 2	= 4 wires
3 posts	2 sets of 2 wires + the end 2	= 6 wires
4 posts	3 sets of 2 wires + the end 2	= 8 wires
n posts	$(n - 1)$ sets of 2 wires + the end 2	$= 2(n - 1) + 2$
		$= 2n$ wires

6.11 INDICES

In the term x^4, the 4 is called the **index** or **exponent** or **power**.

x^4 means $x \times x \times x \times x$,   ie x multiplied by itself 4 times.

There is no equivalent 'common-sense' definition for a negative or fractional power. You use the 4 basic index rules to define them.

6.11.1 The Basic Index Rules

C/G

1.	$a^m \times a^n = a^{m+n}$	2.	$a^m \div a^n = a^{m-n}$
3.	$\left(a^m\right)^n = a^{mn}$	4.	$(ab)^n = a^n b^n$

At the **C/G** level, only the simplest examples using the index rules are included.

eg $\quad x^3 \times x^5 = x^{3+5} = x^8 \qquad \dfrac{x^6}{x^4} = x^{6-4} = x^2$

6.11.2 The Basic Definitions

C

1.	$a^0 = 1$	2.	$a^{-n} = \dfrac{1}{a^n}$
3.	$a^{\frac{1}{n}} = \sqrt[n]{a}$	4.	$a^{\frac{m}{n}} = \sqrt[n]{(a^m)} = \left(\sqrt[n]{a}\right)^m$

6.11.3 Simplifying Indices with Numbers

C

When an index expression is to be evaluated for <u>number</u> values, you should use the definitions to simplify as much as possible first.

It is simpler to evaluate roots <u>before</u> evaluating powers.

Example 1:

$$8^{\frac{1}{3}} = \sqrt[3]{8}$$
$$= 2$$

Example 2:

$$9^{\frac{3}{2}} = \left(\sqrt[2]{9}\right)^3$$
$$= 3^3 = 27$$

Example 3:

$$125^{-\frac{2}{3}} = \frac{1}{125^{\frac{2}{3}}} = \frac{1}{\left(\sqrt[3]{125}\right)^2}$$
$$= \frac{1}{5^2} = \frac{1}{25}$$

6.11.4 Simplifying Indices with Letters

c

When an <u>algebraic</u> index expression is to be simplified, use the basic index rules to simplify as much as possible. All the normal rules of algebra will also apply to index terms.

You may be required to leave an answer with positive powers or roots, or with the index term in the numerator of a fraction.

Example 1:

$$\left(x^{-2}\right)^5$$
$$= x^{-2 \times 5}$$
$$= x^{-10}$$
$$= \frac{1}{x^{10}}$$

Example 2:

$$3x^{\frac{1}{2}}\left(2x^{-2}\right)^3 = 3x^{\frac{1}{2}} \times 2^3 \times x^{-2 \times 3}$$
$$= 3 \times 8 \times x^{\frac{1}{2}} \times x^{-6}$$
$$= 24x^{-6+\frac{1}{2}} = 24x^{-\frac{11}{2}}$$
$$= \frac{24}{\sqrt{x^{11}}}$$

Example 3:

$$x^{\frac{3}{2}}\left(x^{\frac{3}{2}} - x^{-\frac{3}{2}}\right)$$
$$= x^{\frac{3}{2}} \times x^{\frac{3}{2}} - x^{\frac{3}{2}} \times x^{-\frac{3}{2}}$$
$$= x^{\frac{3}{2}+\frac{3}{2}} - x^{-\frac{3}{2}+\frac{3}{2}}$$
$$= x^3 - x^0 = x^3 - 1$$

6.12 FUNCTIONS

6.12.1 Definitions and Notation

A **function** is a mathematical rule which inputs values, acts on them and outputs corresponding values.

If y is the output value for an input value x using a particular function f, you say that
 x **maps onto** y **under** f,   or y **is the image of** x **under** f.
You can write this as:
$$f : x \rightarrow y \qquad \text{or} \qquad y = f(x) \qquad (\text{read } f(x) \text{ as "} f \text{ of } x\text{")}$$

The mathematical rule is usually given using an algebraic expression.

eg $f(x) = 3x - 5$ $g(x) = x^2 - 5x + 2$ $h(x) = \dfrac{3}{x}$

You call this the **formula for** or **the equation of the function**.

When you find the function value for a particular x value a, you say that you are **evaluating** f **for** $x = a$. You use the same methods as in Section 6.1.2.

The set of all input values is called the **domain** of the function.
The set of all output values for that domain is called the **range** of the function.

The domain will often be the set of real numbers. It can also be a finite set of numbers. When you write a finite set of numbers, you show them inside 'curly' brackets, eg **{1, 2, 3}**.

Example 1: What is the range of the function $f(x) = x^2 - 3$,
for the domain $\{-2, -1, 0, 1, 2\}$?

$f(x) = x^2 - 3 \qquad f(-2) = (-2)^2 - 3 = 4 - 3 = 1$

Similarly $\quad f(-1) = -2 \qquad f(0) = -3 \qquad f(1) = -2 \qquad f(2) = 1$

The range is $\{-3, -2, 1\}$.

You can find the x value for a given range value, y, by substituting for y and solving the function equation.

Example 2: If $f(x) = 4x - 5$, find   (a) $f(-2)$,   (b) a when $f(a) = 17$.

(a) $\quad f(x) = 4x - 5$

$\quad f(-2) = 4 \times (-2) - 5$

$\qquad = -8 - 5$

$\qquad = -13$

(b) $\quad f(a) = 17$

$\quad 4a - 5 = 17$

$\quad 4a = 17 + 5$

$\quad 4a = 22$

$\quad a = 5.5$

6.12.2 The Graph of a Function

C/G

You can 'show' a function by plotting the points $(x, f(x))$ where the x coordinate is the domain value and the y coordinate is the corresponding image value.

$y = f(x)$ is **the equation of the graph of the function** f. Functions of a similar form will produce similar shaped graphs.

6.12.3 Linear Functions

C/G

Any function whose equation has the form $f(x) = ax + b$ is called a **linear function**.

The graph of any linear function will be a straight line.

Example: Draw the graph of the function $f(x) = 2x + 2$, ie draw $y = 2x + 2$.

(See Section 4.7 for details on drawing.)

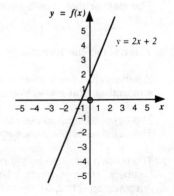

6.12.4 Quadratic Functions

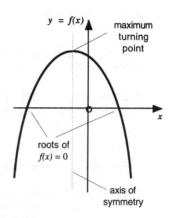

Any function of the form $f(x) = ax^2 + bx + c$
$(a \neq 0)$ is called a **quadratic function**.

The graph of any quadratic function will be a
parabola.

Every parabola is a symmetric curve, with a
vertical **axis of symmetry**. The parabola can
sit U-shaped or upside down U-shaped.

The lowest point on the U-shaped parabola is
called the **minimum turning point**.

The highest point on an upside down U-shaped
parabola is the **maximum turning point**.

A quadratic function can be drawn by plotting some points and drawing the curve
through them, as shown in the example below.

Example: Draw the graph of the function $f(x) = x^2 - 2x - 8$, for $-3 \leq x \leq 5$.
State the equation of the axis of symmetry and the coordinates of
the minimum turning point.

You have to draw $y = x^2 - 2x - 8$.

1. Choose some x values in the domain
   and find the corresponding y values.

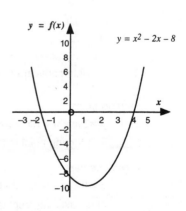

x	-3	-2	-1	0	1	2	3	4	5
y	7	0	-5	-8	-9	-8	-5	0	7

2. Plot these points.

3. Draw a smooth curve through
   the points.

   The axis of symmetry is $x = 1$.
   The minimum turning point is **(1, –9)**.

6.12.5 Sketching Quadratics

If only a rough sketch of the parabola is required, you can obtain that without plotting point by point.

Find the critical points on the parabola, ie the x and y axis intercepts and the turning point.

It is helpful to note that a **positive x^2 term** will give a **U-shape**, and a **negative x^2 term** will give an **upside down U-shape**.

1. Find the x axis intercepts by solving $f(x) = 0$.

2. Find the x coordinate of the turning point. Because of the symmetry of the parabola, it must be halfway between the intercepts. Find the y coordinate of the turning point by substituting in the formula.

3. Find the y axis intercept by evaluating for $x = 0$.

4. Check the sign of the x^2 term.

5. Plot these points and sketch the parabola. Annotate your drawing by showing the values of these points.

Example: Sketch the the graph of the function $f(x) = x^2 - 3x$.

x axis intercepts

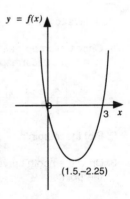

Solve $f(x) = 0$

$$x^2 - 3x = 0$$
$$x(x - 3) = 0$$
$$x = 0 \qquad x - 3 = 0$$
$$x = 3$$

The x axis intercepts are (0,0) and (3,0).

Turning point
$$x = 1.5 \qquad y = 1.5^2 - 3 \times 1.5 = -2.25$$
The turning point is (1.5,–2.25).

y axis intercept
$$x = 0 \qquad y = 0^2 - 3 \times 0 = 0$$
The y axis intercept is (0,0).

6.12.6 Exponential Functions

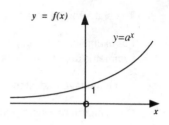

A function of the form

$$f(x) = a^x \qquad (a \text{ is a natural number})$$

is called an **exponential function**.

Since $a^0 = 1$, every exponential function will pass through (0,1), and will have the shape as shown.

6.12.7 Hyperbolic Functions

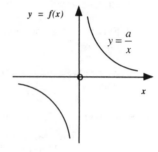

A function of the form

$$f(x) = \frac{a}{x} \qquad (x \neq 0)$$

is called an **hyperbolic function**.

You should be familiar with the function and the shape of its curve, as shown in the diagram.

The name is not required to be known for Standard Grade.

6.12.8 Trigonometric Functions

Any function of the form

$$f(x) = a\sin(bx)^\circ + c \qquad \text{or} \qquad f(x) = a\cos(bx)^\circ + c$$

is called a **trigonometric function**.

See Section 5.8 for further details on such functions, including their graphs.

Example: The depth of water, d m, in a harbour, h hours after noon, is given by the formula:
$$d(h) = 4.5 - 2\cos(30h)^\circ$$

What was the depth of the water at 4 pm that afternoon?

At 4 pm, $h = 4$ $\quad d(4) = 4.5 - 2\cos(30 \times 4)^\circ$

$$= 4.5 - 2\cos(120)^\circ$$

$$= 5.5 \qquad \text{The depth of water was } \textbf{5.5 m.}$$

6.12.9 Finding a Function Formula from a Graph

The shape of the graph may give a clue as to the form of the function formula.

For example, any straight line has an equation of the form $y = ax + b$. A parabola symmetric about the y axis has an equation of the form $y = ax^2 + c$.

You may have to decide this yourself, or the question may give this information.

Only linear functions are included at the **C/G** level. Other functions are at the **C** level.

To find the equation of a function:

1. Choose any 2 points from the graph - take the simplest coordinates you can.

2. Substitute the coordinates into the formula for the function to get 2 equations in 2 unknowns.

3. Solve these simultaneously to find a and b and therefore the formula of the equation.

Example: f is a function with formula $f(x) = ax^2 + b$.

The graph of the function is shown opposite.
Find the equation of the function f.

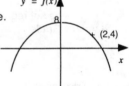

$$f(x) = ax^2 + b$$

At $(0,8)$ $\quad 8 = a \times 0^2 + b$

$\qquad\qquad b = 8 \quad$ **Equation 1**

At $(2,4)$ $\quad 4 = a \times 2^2 + b$

$\qquad\qquad 4a + b = 4 \quad$ **Equation 2**

Solving equations **1** and **2** simultaneously gives: $\quad a = -1, \ b = 8$
(See Section 6.8 for the method.)

So $\qquad f(x) = -x^2 + 8 \qquad$ or $\qquad f(x) = 8 - x^2$

6.13 PROPORTION

6.13.1 Direct Proportion   Ⓖ

T is **directly proportional** to s if, as s increases, T increases proportionally, eg as s doubles, T also doubles, etc.

In practice, you can recognise and use direct proportion by making use of any of the following:

1. The **graph** of values (s, T) will give a **straight line through (0,0)**.

   (The gradient of the line will be $\dfrac{T}{s}$.)

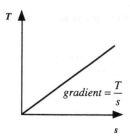

$$gradient = \frac{T}{s}$$

2. **The Constant Ratio Principle**

   The ratio $\dfrac{T}{s}$ is the same for every pair of corresponding values s and T.

3. **The Multiplier Principle**

   If s and T are any pair of corresponding values and $s' = ks$ for any constant k, then $T' = kT$ is the corresponding value to s'.

Example: Are the quantities P and Q, as shown in the table, in direct proportion?

Q	2.5	6	10
P	17.5	42	65

Using the Constant Ratio Principle:

You must check the ratio for every pair of values.

$$\frac{P_1}{Q_1} = \frac{17.5}{2.5} = 7 \qquad \frac{P_2}{Q_2} = \frac{42}{6} = 7 \qquad \frac{P_3}{Q_3} = \frac{65}{10} = 6.5$$

Since the ratio is not always the same, the quantities are **not** in direct proportion.

Using the Multiplier Principle:

$$\frac{Q_3}{Q_2} = \frac{10}{6} = 1.66... \quad \text{ie } Q_3 = 1.66... \times Q_2$$

$$\frac{P_3}{P_2} = \frac{65}{42} = 1.54... \quad \text{ie } P_3 = 1.54... \times P_2$$

Since the multiplier is not the same, the quantities are **not** in direct proportion.

6.13.2 Inverse Proportion

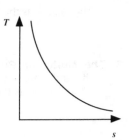

T is **inversely proportional** to s if, as s increases, T decreases proportionally, eg as s doubles, T halves, etc.

In practice, you can recognise and use inverse proportion by making use of any of the following:

1. The **graph** of values (s, T) will give a hyperbolic curve.

   From the graph, you can see that as one quantity increases, the other decreases.

2. **The Constant Product Principle**
   The product sT is the same for every pair of corresponding values s and T.

3. **The Inverse Multiplier Principle**
   If s and T are any pair of corresponding values and $s' = ks$ for any constant k, then $T' = \frac{T}{k}$ is the corresponding value to s'.

(G)

6.13.3 Examples Using Proportion

There are a variety of approaches to proportion questions using the above ideas.

However most people set out proportion examples along the following lines (based on the multiplier principle). These guidelines will work for either direct or inverse proportion.

1. Show the two quantities being compared as headings.
   Make sure that the quantity being looked for is on the right.

2. Find a corresponding pair of values and enter these in the first line.

3. Enter the other 'known' quantity on the left of the second line.

4. Decide whether the expected answer should be more or less than the right hand value.

5. Set up a ratio (fraction) using the 2 values in the left hand column:

   If you want **more**, make the fraction greater than 1, ie **bigger over smaller**.

   If you want **less**, make the fraction less than 1, ie **smaller over bigger**.

6. Multiply the right hand value by the fraction.

Example 1:

35 books cost £157.50.
How much will 55 cost?

books		cost(£)
35	$\rightarrow$	157.50
55	$\rightarrow$	more

$$\frac{55}{35} \times 157.50$$
$$= 247.50$$

55 books will cost **£247.50**.

Example 2:

9 men complete a task in 5 hours.
How long will 15 men take?

men		hours
9	$\rightarrow$	5
15	$\rightarrow$	less

$$\frac{9}{15} \times 5$$
$$= 3$$

15 men will take **3 hours**.

6.13.4 The Unitary Method for Direct Proportion Ⓖ

Problems involving direct proportion can also be worked out by finding the value for one item first.

This is a simpler approach which avoids setting up the ratio directly. However, it is really only useful with simple direct proportion.

Example (see Example 1 in 6.13.3 above):

books		cost(£)	
35	$\rightarrow$	157.50	
1	$\rightarrow$	$\dfrac{157.50}{35}$	$= 4.5$
55	$\rightarrow$	55×4.5	$= 247.50$

55 books will cost **£247.50**

6.14 VARIATION

It is often helpful to describe relationships between quantities using the algebraic language of variation.

This allows us to describe the relationship in the form of a **variation statement** using the variation symbol α.

This can be changed into an equation, the **variation equation**.

Although there are different types of variation, the approach to most of the questions is the same:

1. Write down the variation statement from the information given in the question.

2. Change to a variation equation by replacing the variation sign by an equals sign and a constant, the **variation constant**.

Variation statement	$P \propto Q$
Variation equation	$P = kQ$

3. Use a set of corresponding values given in the question to find a value for k.

4. Rewrite the variation equation <u>using the number value for the constant k</u>.

5. Use this equation to find out any other value required.

G

6.14.1 Direct Variation

If P varies directly as Q, then P is directly proportional to Q.

The different methods of using direct proportion identified in Section 6.13.1 will also hold for direct variation therefore.

In particular, direct variation can be identified by the straight line graph through the origin.

Example 1: P varies directly as Q. If $P = 240$ when $Q = 40$, give an equation linking P to Q and hence find P when $Q = 65$.

Variation statement $\qquad P \propto Q$

Variation equation $\qquad P = kQ$

Substitute corresponding pair of values

$$240 = k \times 40$$
$$k = \frac{240}{40} = 6$$

Rewrite variation equation

$$P = 6Q$$

Use this equation with $Q = 65$,

$$P = 6 \times 65$$
$$= 390$$

A variation statement can also be written linking powers or roots of quantities in the same way.

In this case, it is the power or root of the quantity that would be used to check the Multiplier or Ratio Principle, or to produce a straight line graph.

Example 2: T varies directly as the square of r. If $T = 20$ when $r = 4$, find the equation of variation and hence find r when $T = 11.25$.

$$T \propto r^2$$
$$T = kr^2$$
$$20 = k \times 4^2 \qquad\qquad T = 11.25, \qquad 11.25 = 1.25r^2$$
$$k = \frac{20}{16} = 1.25 \qquad\qquad\qquad\qquad r^2 = \frac{11.25}{1.25} = 9$$
$$T = 1.25r^2 \qquad\qquad\qquad\qquad r = \sqrt{9} = 3$$

6.14.2 Inverse Variation

If P varies inversely as Q, then P is inversely proportional to Q.

The different methods of using inverse proportion identified in Section 6.13.2 will therefore also hold for inverse variation.

In particular, inverse variation can be identified by the hyperbola shaped graph. Inverse variation is always signalled by "1 over the quantity".

Example 1: P varies inversely as Q. If $P = 25$ when $Q = 10$, find the equation of variation and hence find P when $Q = 75$.

$$P \propto \frac{1}{Q}$$

$$P = \frac{k}{Q}$$

$$25 = \frac{k}{10}$$

$$k = 10 \times 25 = 250$$

$$\boldsymbol{P = \frac{250}{Q}}$$

$$Q = 75, \qquad P = \frac{250}{75}$$

$$P = 3.33...$$

$$P = \boldsymbol{3.3} \text{ to 1 dp}$$

$$\left(\text{or } P = \frac{250}{75} = \frac{10}{3} = 3\tfrac{1}{3} \right)$$

A variation statement can also be written linking powers or roots of quantities in the same way.

In this case, it is the power or root of the quantity that would be used to check the Inverse Multiplier or Product Principle, or to produce a hyperbola graph.

Example 2: S varies inversely as the square root of a. If $S = 10$ when $a = 4$, find the equation of variation and hence find a when $S = 4$.

$$S \propto \frac{1}{\sqrt{a}}$$

$$S = \frac{k}{\sqrt{a}}$$

$$10 = \frac{k}{\sqrt{4}}$$

$$k = 10 \times \sqrt{4} = 20$$

$$S = \frac{20}{\sqrt{a}}$$

$$S = 4, \qquad 4 = \frac{20}{\sqrt{a}}$$

$$4\sqrt{a} = 20$$

$$\sqrt{a} = \frac{20}{4} = 5$$

$$a = 5^2 = \boldsymbol{25}$$

C

6.14.3 Joint Variation

Often a quantity will vary depending on more than one other quantity. This is called **joint variation**.

You set up the statement as before with all **direct** variation quantities on the **top** line and **inverse** variation quantities on the **bottom** line.
You only use one constant for the whole statement.

Example 1: P varies jointly as a and the square root of b. If $P = 25$ when $a = 5$ and $b = 4$, find the equation of variation and hence find P when $a = 2$ and $b = 16$.

$$P \propto a\sqrt{b}$$
$$P = ka\sqrt{b}$$
$$25 = k \times 5 \times \sqrt{4}$$
$$k = \frac{25}{10} = 2.5$$
$$\boldsymbol{P = 2.5a\sqrt{b}}$$

$a = 2, \quad b = 16$
$$P = 2.5 \times 2 \times \sqrt{16}$$
$$= 20$$

Example 2: P varies directly as the cube of a and inversely as the square root of b. If $P = 10$ when $a = 2$ and $b = 16$, find the equation of variation and hence find a when $P = 27$ and $b = 25$.

$$P \propto \frac{a^3}{\sqrt{b}}$$
$$P = k\frac{a^3}{\sqrt{b}}$$
$$10 = k\frac{2^3}{\sqrt{16}}$$
$$10 \times 4 = k \times 8$$
$$k = \frac{40}{8} = 5$$
$$\boldsymbol{P = 5\frac{a^3}{\sqrt{b}}}$$

$P = 27, \quad b = 25$
$$27 = 5\frac{a^3}{\sqrt{25}}$$
$$27 \times 5 = 5a^3$$
$$a^3 = 27$$
$$\boldsymbol{a = \sqrt[3]{27} = 3}$$

6.14.4 Graphs of Variation (or Proportion)

Direct Variation (Proportion)

- always gives a straight line through the origin, with gradient $\dfrac{P}{Q}$.

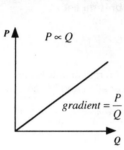

If $P \propto Q^2$, the graph of P against Q^2 would give a straight line, although the graph of P against Q would give a curve.

Inverse Variation (Proportion) C/G

- always gives a hyperbola shaped curve.

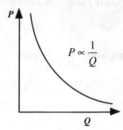

The graph of P against $\dfrac{1}{Q}$ would give a straight line.

6.14.5 Effect of a Change in Variable

Questions involving changes in variables are solved by the same method as shown in Section 6.10.3.

Example: P varies jointly as a and the square of b.
What is the effect on P of doubling both a and b?

$$P \propto ab^2$$
$$P = kab^2$$
$$a \to 2a \qquad b \to 2b \qquad P \to P'$$
$$P' = k(2a)(2b)^2$$
$$= k \times 2a \times 4b^2$$
$$= 8(kab^2)$$
$$= 8P \qquad \text{P becomes \textbf{8 times as big}.}$$

7. STATISTICS

7.1 ANALYSING A DATA SET

A group of values is called a **data set.**

7.1.1 The Mean (often called the **average**)

The mean is the average of all the values in the data set. To find the mean:

1. Add up all the values in the data set.

2. Divide by the number of values in the data set.

7.1.2 The Median

The median is the middle value in the data set when the values are listed in order of size. If there is an even number of values in the data set the median will be the mean of the middle pair.

You must arrange all the values in order of size first.

7.1.3 The Mode

The mode is the most frequently occurring value(s) in the data set.

7.1.4 The Range

The range is a measure of the spread of values in the data set.

$$\boxed{\textbf{range} = \textbf{maximum} - \textbf{minimum}}$$

Example: The following scores were obtained by pupils of 1A in a test.

5	5	8	8	9	3	8	10	7	7
6	6	3	8	6	8	4	5	6	5

Find the mean, median, mode and range for the data set.

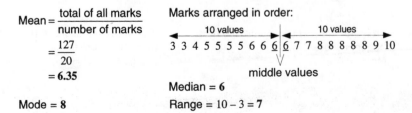

$$\text{Mean} = \frac{\text{total of all marks}}{\text{number of marks}}$$

$$= \frac{127}{20}$$

$$= 6.35$$

Mode = **8**

Marks arranged in order:

◄——— 10 values ———►◄——— 10 values ———►
3 3 4 5 5 5 5 6 6 <u>6</u>|<u>6</u> 7 7 8 8 8 8 8 9 10

middle values

Median = **6**

Range = $10 - 3 = \textbf{7}$

7.2 USING A FREQUENCY TABLE

A data set can be shown in a **frequency table**. Sometimes the information may be presented in this form initially.

The data set for the Example in Section 7.1 can be represented as follows.

Score	Tally	Frequency	Score x Frequency	Cumulative Frequency
3	I I	2	6	2
4	I	1	4	3
5	I I I I	4	20	7
6	I I I I	4	24	11
7	I I	2	14	13
8	+++T	5	40	18
9	I	1	9	19
10	I	1	10	20
TOTAL		20	127	

It is helpful to include a **Tally** column when creating a frequency table from unordered data. The **Score x Frequency** column is useful when calculating the mean (see below).

The **Cumulative Frequency** column gives a 'running total' of the frequencies. It is only required at the **C/G** level and can be useful for finding the median and the quartiles from a frequency table (see Section 7.3).

Example: Find the mean, median, mode and range from the frequency table above.

$$\text{Mean} = \frac{\text{Total of Score x Frequency column}}{\text{Total of Frequency column}}$$

$$= \frac{127}{20}$$

$$= 6.35$$

From the Frequency column, the most frequent score is 8.
Mode = **8**

From the Cumulative Frequency column, the 10th and 11th scores are both 6.
Median = **6**

The maximum score is 10 and the minimum score is 3.
Range = $10 - 3 = 7$

7.3 QUARTILES AND SEMI-INTERQUARTILE RANGE

A data set is divided into two sets of equal size by the **median**. The medians of these sets are called the **quartiles** - the **lower quartile** and the **upper quartile**.
It is common to use the notation Q_1 for the lower quartile, Q_2 for the median and Q_3 for the upper quartile.

If there is an even number of values in the set, the quartile is the mean of the middle two values.

The **semi-interquartile range** is another measure of the spread of values in the data set.

$$\text{Semi-interquartile range} = \frac{\text{upper quartile} - \text{lower quartile}}{2}$$

Example 1: Find the median, lower quartile, upper quartile and semi-interquartile range for the scores listed below obtained by pupils of 1A.

5	5	8	8	9	3	8	10	7	7
6	6	3	8	6	8	4	5	6	5

Marks arranged in order:

10 values | 10 values

3 3 4 5 5 | 5 5 6 6 6 | 6 7 7 8 8 | 8 8 8 9 10

5 values | 5 values | 5 values | 5 values

$Q_1 = 5$ $Q_2 = 6$ $Q_3 = 8$

Semi-interquartile range

$$= \frac{\text{upper quartile} - \text{lower quartile}}{2}$$

$$= \frac{8 - 5}{2}$$

$$= 1.5$$

Example 2: Find the median, lower quartile, upper quartile and semi-interquartile range for the scores listed below obtained by pupils of 1B.

5	8	9	3	8	7	7
6	3	8	4	6	5	

Marks arranged in order:

6 values | 6 values

3 3 4 | 5 5 6 (6) 7 7 8 | 8 8 9

3 values | 3 values | 3 values | 3 values

$Q_1 = 4.5$ $Q_2 = 6$ $Q_3 = 8$

Semi-interquartile range

$$= \frac{\text{upper quartile} - \text{lower quartile}}{2}$$

$$= \frac{8 - 4.5}{2}$$

$$= 1.75$$

7.4 STANDARD DEVIATION

C/G

The **standard deviation** is a measure of how the values in a data set differ from the mean value. A larger standard deviation indicates a greater spread in the values.

Most of the data used at Standard Grade will be obtained as a random sample from a larger population. You use the formula for the **sample standard deviation**, s, therefore.

$$s = \sqrt{\frac{\sum (x - \bar{x})^2}{n-1}} = \sqrt{\frac{\sum x^2 - \frac{(\sum x)^2}{n}}{n-1}}$$

where $\bar{x}$ is the mean, n is the sample size, $\sum x$ is the sum of all the data values and $\sum x^2$ is the sum of the squares of all the data values.

The second version is easier to compute and avoids the possibility of rounding errors.

Example: The following scores were obtained by some S1 pupils in a test.

5	5	8	8	9	3	8	10	7	7
6	6	3	8	6	8	4	5	6	5

Find the sample standard deviation for the data set.

$$\sum x^2 = 877$$
$$\sum x = 127$$
$$n = 20$$

$$s = \sqrt{\frac{\sum x^2 - \frac{(\sum x)^2}{n}}{n-1}} = \sqrt{\frac{877 - \frac{127^2}{20}}{20-1}}$$
$$= 1.926...$$
$$= \mathbf{1.93} \quad \text{to 2 dp}$$

7.5 GRAPHS AND CHARTS

7.5.1 Different Forms of Graphs and Charts

G C/G

A data set is often presented in a picture form which you must interpret, or you may wish to represent the data set in such a way yourself.

There are different ways of representing the same information. The choice of format depends on the nature of the data and what you wish to do with the information. The following examples illustrate some of the common methods used.

Example 1: The pupils in a class of 30 pupils recorded their shoe size. The information was recorded in a table:

shoe size	1	2	3	4	5	6
frequency	3	10	6	4	6	1

Bar Chart

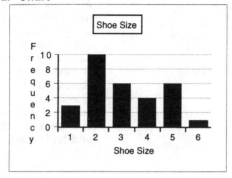

A bar chart gives an effective way of showing the relative sizes of each quantity. It is particularly useful for **discrete** data, ie where the data values can only take certain values and not any value in between. For example, there is no shoe size of 2.65.

Line Graph

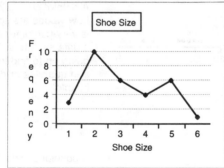

A line graph is particularly useful for showing trends in a graph.
If the data values can take any value, or gradually change, you say the data is **continuous**. For example, a person's height changes continuously. So for a graph of "height at a particular age", it may be more appropriate to draw a smooth curve through the points.

Pie Chart

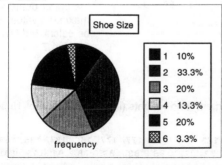

A pie chart is particularly useful for showing how each part compares both to the others and to the whole. You can see immediately in this example, that about one third of the pupils have shoe size 2.
Pie charts are harder to construct and the method is shown in Section 7.5.2.

Example 2: The following scores were obtained by pupils of 2A in a test.

25	35	18	8	39	13	18	10	7	27
26	26	33	28	16	18	24	15	16	25

Stem-and-Leaf Diagram

```
              Test Score
    0 | 7 8
    1 | 0 3 5 6 6 8 8 8        where  2|4
    2 | 4 5 5 6 6 7 8          represents a score
    3 | 3 5 9                  of 24
    |    |
   stem  leaves                n = 20
```

A stem-and-leaf diagram is useful when the data can be separated into groups.
In this case the tens digit for each score is in the 'stem' and the units digit for each score forms the 'leaves'.
A second data set can be added to the left of the stem in a **'back-to-back' stem-and-leaf diagram.**

C/G

Dotplot

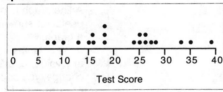

A dotplot shows you quickly how values are spread out. It is very useful for rearranging a data set into order and for going on to find the median and quartiles or drawing a boxplot.

C/G

Boxplot

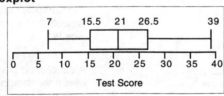

A boxplot shows the spread of the results by identifying the minimum value, the lower quartile, the median, the upper quartile and the maximum value. These must be calculated first. See Section 7.5.3.

Example 3: The heights (in cm) and weights (in kg) of a group of 15 people were recorded.

height	161	163	165	169	173	173	175	177	177	181	184	185	189	191	194
weight	65	61	69	69	73	79	85	83	89	78	91	96	101	96	104

Scattergraph

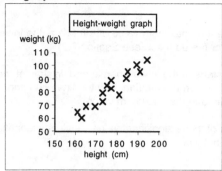

A scattergraph is useful for showing the relationship between two quantities. In this example, each point represents the height and weight of an individual.

When the points plotted lie closely around a straight line, you say there is a **strong correlation** between the two quantities. See Section 7.5.5.

7.5.2 Constructing a Pie Chart

1. Find the total number of items in the data set.

2. Find what fraction of the total data is contained in each category.

3. EITHER   Convert each fraction to a percentage and use a pie chart scale to draw the chart.

    OR   Find how many degrees there are in that fraction of 360°, and use a protractor / angle measurer to draw the chart.

Example: For the information given in Example 1 in Section 7.5.1, find what size of sector would represent pupils with shoe size 4.

$$\text{Total number of pupils} = 30$$

$$\text{Pupils with shoe size } 4 = 4$$

$$\text{Fraction of pupils} = \frac{4}{30}$$

EITHER

$$\frac{4}{30} = 0.133... = 13.3\%$$

Use a pie chart scale to draw a sector of **13.3%**.

OR

$$\frac{4}{30} \times 360 = 48$$

Use a protractor / angle measurer to draw an angle of **48°**.

7.5.3 Constructing a Boxplot

C/G

1. Find the minimum value, the maximum value, the median, the lower quartile and the upper quartile for the data set (see Section 7.3).

2. Draw the box so that it starts at the lower quartile and finishes at the upper quartile. The centre line sits on the median, and the lines on either side come out to the minimum value and the maximum value.

3. It is important that each of these significant values is clearly identified on the diagram (see Example below).

Example: Draw a boxplot to show the information given in Example 2 in Section 7.5.1.

Data arranged in order:

7 8 10 13 15 | 16 16 18 18 18 | 24 25 25 26 26 | 27 28 33 35 39

$$Q_1 = \frac{15+16}{2} \qquad Q_2 = \frac{18+24}{2} \qquad Q_3 = \frac{26+27}{2}$$

$$= 15.5 \qquad\qquad = 21 \qquad\qquad = 26.5$$

minimum = 7   maximum = 39

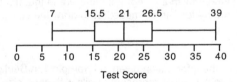

Test Score

7.5.4 Trends in a Graph

G

The **trend** in a graph refers to what is happening on the whole, without worrying about small ups and down.

The overall trend is decreasing.

The overall trend is rising and then falling.

7.5.5 The Best-Fitting Straight Line on a Scattergraph

When there is a strong correlation (see Section 7.5.1) between the variables in a scattergraph, it will be possible to draw a straight line passing through the points so that the points are grouped as closely as possible around it.
You call this the **best-fitting straight line**.

If the gradient of this line is positive, you say there is a **positive correlation** between the variables. If the gradient is negative, you say there is a **negative correlation** between the variables.

At the **G** level, you only need to draw the line. At the **C/G** level, you must be able to find the equation of the line.

You can find the equation of this line as follows.

1. Draw the best-fitting straight line through the points.

2. Choose any two points on the line.

3. Find the gradient of the line using these points.

4. Substitute the gradient and the coordinates of one of the points into the standard equation of a straight line, $y = mx + c$, to find the equation of the line.

Example: For the data set in Example 3 in Section 7.5.1, draw the best-fitting straight line and find the equation of this line.

The best-fitting line has been sketched. It passes through the points (160,60) and (200,110).

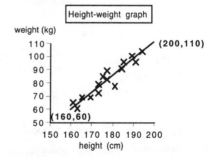

Height-weight graph

gradient $m = \dfrac{110 - 60}{200 - 160}$

$= \dfrac{50}{40}$

$= 1.25$

$y = mx + c$

$60 = 1.25 \times 160 + c$

$c = 60 - 1.25 \times 160$

$= -140$

Equation of Line: $y = 1.25x - 140$

ie   **weight** $= 1.25 \times$ **height** $- 140$

7.6 PROBABILITY

Probability is a measure of how likely an event is to happen. It is measured on a scale of 0 (impossible) to 1 (certain). Probabilities can be given as common fractions, decimal fractions or percentages.

Probabilities for certain events can be **calculated theoretically**. To do this you must know how many possible outcomes there are and whether they are equally likely.

Probabilities for events can also be **determined experimentally** by analysing previous events. The likelihood of rain tomorrow can be predicted based on what has happened previously.

7.6.1 Calculating Probability Theoretically

At the **G** level, you should be able to state the probability of a simple outcome, eg throwing a 6 on a normal dice. Most of the work will be at the **C/G** level.

The probability of an event occurring, P(event), is given by

$$P(event) = \frac{\text{number of favourable outcomes}}{\text{total number of outcomes}}$$

where all the outcomes are equally likely.

Example 1: What is the probability of throwing (a) a 6, and (b) an even number on an ordinary dice?

(a) $P(event) = \dfrac{\text{number of favourable outcomes}}{\text{total number of outcomes}}$ Favourable outcome is a 6.
6 possible outcomes.

$P(6) = \dfrac{1}{6}$

(b) $P(event) = \dfrac{\text{number of favourable outcomes}}{\text{total number of outcomes}}$ Favourable outcomes are 2, 4 or 6.
6 possible outcomes.

$P(even) = \dfrac{3}{6} = \dfrac{1}{2}$

Example 2: What is the probability of picking an ace from a pack of cards?

$P(event) = \dfrac{\text{number of favourable outcomes}}{\text{total number of outcomes}}$ Favourable outcomes are 4 aces.
52 possible outcomes
(52 cards in the pack).

$P(ace) = \dfrac{4}{52} = \dfrac{1}{13}$

7.6.2 Determining Probability Experimentally

If an experiment is carried out repeatedly, the **relative frequency** of a particular outcome can be calculated.

$$\text{relative frequency} = \frac{\textbf{number of occurences of the outcome}}{\textbf{total number of trials}}$$

The relative frequency is an estimate of the probability of that particular outcome occurring. As the total number of trials increases, the estimate of the probability improves.

Example 1: In a survey of 50 pupils, 35 said they liked the music of Normandy Arrows.
(a) What is the probability that a pupil chosen at random would like the music of Normandy Arrows?
There are 1200 pupils in the school.
(b) If this sample is representative of all the pupils in the school, how many pupils would you expect to like Normandy Arrows?

(a) $\text{relative frequency} = \dfrac{\text{number of occurences of the outcome}}{\text{total number of trials}}$

$$= \frac{35}{50} = \frac{7}{10}$$

P(pupil likes Normandy Arrows) $= \dfrac{\textbf{7}}{\textbf{10}}$

(b) Number of pupils who like Normandy Arrows $= \dfrac{7}{10} \times 1200$

$$= \textbf{840}$$

Example 2: The following scores were obtained by some S1 pupils in a test.

5	5	8	8	9	3	8	10	7	7
6	6	3	8	6	8	4	5	6	5

What is the probability that an S1 pupil chosen at random scored more than 5 in the test?

$\text{relative frequency} = \dfrac{\text{number of occurences of the outcome}}{\text{total number of trials}}$

$$= \frac{13}{20} = 0.65$$

P(score > 5) $= \textbf{0.65}$

8. PROBLEM SOLVING

Problem solving lies at the heart of mathematics. All maths questions involve some problem solving but Reasoning and Enquiry (**R&E**) questions usually involve more complex types of problems. This chapter concentrates on this kind of question.

An attempt has been made to identify different <u>types</u> of R&E questions which often appear in the exams. Although examples have been used to illustrate a particular type of question, they often overlap with other types.

The examples given in this chapter will <u>not</u> cover all possible R&E questions. The contexts will always be different, so the questions will look different . However the maths being used will be similar. The examples here will illustrate the general approaches required.

The level of a question is likely to depend more on the maths involved than the type of R&E question. In this chapter, questions have been identified as either at **Credit** or **General** Level. (It is not easy to identify the **C/G** level for this type of question.)

Additional comments to help you understand the solutions have been shown in bold italics like this.

8.1 GENERAL APPROACHES TO PROBLEM SOLVING QUESTIONS

8.1.1 Hints on Tackling Problem Solving Questions   (G)

Showing Working: You must show your working in all maths questions. However in R&E questions, the examiner is looking for particular evidence of how you approached a problem, so it is even more important to explain what you are doing clearly. This will not normally require a lot of writing - just a few words of explanation to accompany your calculations will often be sufficient.

Using a Diagram: In many questions, particularly in trigonometry or geometry, a diagram helps to clarify what information you have and what is required. If the diagram starts to get complicated, then isolate the particular part you require, eg a right angled triangle.

Rounding: You will often have to make your own decision about how to round off an answer. Make use of the other information in the question to decide what would be an appropriate level of accuracy, and keep all rounding until the end of the question (see Section 1.4 for details on rounding).

Answering Mathematically: Questions will be asked which require a YES / NO answer or require you to make a choice, eg as to best value. If you answer these without some mathematical working to support your answer, you are likely to get no marks. Remember it is a <u>mathematics</u> exam your are sitting! In your conclusion, you must show any comparison made to support your answer (see Example 5 in Section 8.2.3).

8.1.2 Useful Techniques for Problem Solving

Try Some Simple Cases: If you are asked to give an answer to a complicated question, start by looking first at some simple cases which are easy to deal with. Use any patterns in the answers to predict an answer to the difficult question.

Trial and Error / Trial and Improvement: You may not be able to find a solution to a problem by any mathematical method that you know. In this case, try out a value - if it does not lead to a solution directly, the answer it gives may help you to predict a better choice for the solution.

Organised Listing: Often problems may involve finding or checking through a list of possibilities. You must be careful to deal with the list in some order - it avoids missing some or double-counting.

Make a Table: Whenever you have a few results, put them into a table in an organised form. It is much easier to spot a pattern when all the values are organised together in front of you.

Spotting Patterns: Once you have some results organised in front of you, look for any patterns in the data. This may involve finding a rule for working out the values, noticing a particular form the answers take, or looking for something that all the values have in common. You must explain your thinking clearly.

Generalise: If you are asked to find a rule, it is important to try and give it in a generalised form using symbols if you can (see Section 6.10.5).

8.1.3 Conjectures and Testing

Mathematicians often extend their knowledge by making **conjectures** (predictions or theories) about a result. They first look at some examples (**particular cases**) and use these to try and spot any patterns in these results which will help them to predict an overall rule or result which is true for all values (**general case**).

This then must be tested further to see if it appears to hold, and, if possible, be proved. Only once a result has been <u>proved</u>, is it formally accepted and it is then known as a **theorem**. No amount of testing will replace a proof in establishing a mathematical result. However, the more testing you do, the more confident you become that the conjecture is true.

In Standard Grade, it is usually acceptable to test for **two further cases** as an indication that you recognise the need to test a conjecture. These must not be values that you have already used in setting up the conjecture.

This approach is useful when investigating a result. However, in a Standard Grade exam, if you are asked to prove a result, testing a conjecture like this will not normally be an acceptable alternative (see Section 8.3).

8.2 MATHEMATICAL MODELLING

Mathematical modelling lies at the heart of many problem solving questions, and allows us to use maths to find an answer to a real-life problem.

The following diagram illustrates the process.

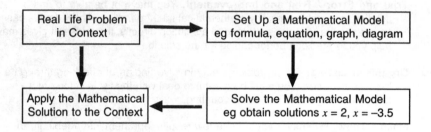

Your aim is to find a 'real-life' solution to a 'real-life' problem. To do this:

1. Set up a **mathematical model** by using some mathematics to describe the situation. A mathematical model can use any of the maths you know - algebra, eg an equation or a formula; geometry, eg Pythagoras in a right angled triangle or a sector of a circle; trigonometry in a triangle; a graph, etc.

   If you introduce letters, you must identify clearly what they represent.

   The setting up of the model will often involve some approximating or assumptions.

   For example, you may have to assume that the ground is perfectly flat and horizontal and a pole is exactly vertical to allow you to model a situation with a right angled triangle. It is important to be aware of any assumptions made.

2. Apply the mathematical facts, concepts and skills relevant to the model to find a **mathematical solution**. At this stage you will make use of the material from the other 7 chapters of this book.

3. It is possible to have a solution to the mathematical model which is not a solution to the problem in context. It is important at the **Credit** Level to specifically rule out any non-valid solutions <u>and</u> explain why.

   For example, a quadratic equation may have 2 solutions, one positive and one negative. In the context, a negative solution may not be a valid solution.

   Always answer a question <u>in its context</u>. For example "$x = 2.5$" is unlikely to be a sufficient solution. Your answer should state what the x represents.

8.2.1 Modelling With a Formula

Example 1: Finding a Formula
At a banquet, tables are arranged in a line as shown.
Each table can sit 2 people on each side and one at each end.

(a) Complete the table to show the number of people that can be seated.

Number of Tables T	1	2	3	4	5	6
Number of People N		10				

(b) Write a formula for the number of people, N, that can be seated at T tables.

(c) Each table is 2 m long, and an extra metre is required at each end of the row of tables for the end chairs. How many people can be seated at a single row of tables in a room of length 45 m?

Solution:
(a) *Complete the table, first for the examples given, and then extend to the other values. Look for patterns in the values - the numbers go up by 4 each time.*
Check by drawing that this rule does work.

Number of Tables T	1	2	3	4	5	6
Number of People N	6	10	14	18	22	26

Check:

4 tables:**18 people**

(b) N values increase by 4 each time, so try '$T \times 4$' in the formula. This always gives 2 less than the N number, so
$N = T \times 4 + 2$ or $N = 4T + 2$.

(c) Length of room = 45 m
Room for chairs = 2 m Amount left = 43 m
Number of tables = $43 \div 2 = 21$ with 1 m left over.
You cannot have half of a table so it is not 21.5!

Use formula for $T = 21$, $N = 21 \times 4 + 2 = 84 + 2 = 86$

Apply your answer back into the context, not just "N = 86"!

86 people can be seated at a single row of tables.

Example 2: Finding a Formula

C

The car allowances for employees of the Driveabout Company are shown in the table.

Engine Size (in cc)	Basic Allowance (up to 100 miles)	Extra Miles (beyond 100)	Extra Miles (beyond 300)
≥ 2000	£25	28p per mile	25p per mile
≥ 1500	£22	25p per mile	22p per mile
< 1500	£20	22p per mile	20p per mile

Write down a formula for the total allowance due, £A, to an employee who has driven n miles, where $100 < n < 200$, in a car with an 1800cc engine.

Solution:

Questions of this type often first involve choosing the appropriate information from a choice of values in a table.

1800cc car : basic allowance of £22
25p per mile for every mile <u>beyond</u> 100, since $100 < n < 200$

Total mileage $= n$ Mileage beyond 100 $= n - 100$

Allowance for extra miles $= (n - 100) \times 25$ p $= 0.25(n - 100)$ in £

Total allowance in £, $A = 22 + 0.25(n - 100)$
$$= 22 + 0.25n - 25$$
$$= 0.25n - 3$$

Always simplify an algebraic expression as far as possible.

The formula for the total allowance in this case is $A = 0.25n - 3$.

Example 3: Finding the Coefficients in a Given Formula

C

The first 3 patterns in a sequence are:

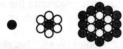

The number of circles, C, required to make the nth pattern is given by
$C = an(n-1) + b$.

(a) Find the values of a and b.

(b) Can a pattern be made using exactly 331 circles? Justify your answer.

Solution:

(a) Using the first pattern $n = 1, C = 1$
$$1 = a \times 1 \times (1-1) + b \quad \text{ie} \quad \mathbf{b = 1}$$

Using the second pattern $n = 2, C = 7$
$$7 = a \times 2 \times (2-1) + b \quad \text{ie} \quad 2a + b = 7$$

Substituting $b = 1$ into $2a + b = 7$
$$2a + 1 = 7$$
$$2a = 6$$
$$\mathbf{a = 3}$$

(b) Substituting $a = 3$ and $b = 1$ into $C = an(n-1) + b$
gives $C = 3n(n-1) + 1$.

If $C = 331$ then
$$3n(n-1) + 1 = 331$$
$$3n^2 - 3n - 330 = 0$$
$$3(n^2 - n - 110) = 0$$
$$3(n-11)(n+10) = 0$$

$n - 11 = 0$ $n + 10 = 0$

$n = 11$ $n = -10$

$n = -10$ is not a valid solution in the context since the number of circles cannot be negative.

$n = 11$ is a valid solution.

A pattern **can** be made using exactly 331 circles.
It would be the 11th pattern in the sequence.

8.2.2 Modelling with "Show that ..." Questions.

Some of the **Credit** Level equation or formula questions in particular involve showing that a particular result holds.

It is important in these questions that you **'start from scratch'**, using whatever maths you can in the situation, and work towards producing the result.
Do <u>not</u> start with the result and try to explain where it came from.

Note that in this type of question, the result is often given. This allows you to attempt the rest of the question even if you could not do the 'show that ...' part.
Do <u>not</u> give up on the whole question.

Note: The following example illustrates the use of **trial and error / improvement** to find a solution when no other method is known.

Example 4:

C

A rectangular sheet of paper measures x cm long and y cm high.

Another rectangle is produced by cutting 1 cm off the top and bottom of the sheet and 2 cm off each side as shown.

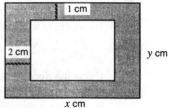

(a) Show that the area, A cm^2, of paper cut off is
$A = 2x + 4y - 8$.

(b) If the area cut off is less than 20 cm^2, and x and y are integers, list all the possible values for x and y.

Solution:

Length of small rectangle $= x - 2 - 2 = x - 4$
Height of small rectangle $= y - 1 - 1 = y - 2$

Area of small rectangle $= (x - 4)(y - 2)$
Area of big rectangle $= xy$

Area cut off = area of big rectangle − area of small rectangle
$$A = xy - (x - 4)(y - 2)$$
$$A = xy - (xy - 2x - 4y + 8)$$
$$A = xy - xy + 2x + 4y - 8$$
$$\mathbf{A = 2x + 4y - 8}$$

(b) To allow edges to be cut off, $x > 4$ and $y > 2$. Check out values above that.

Make sure you work systematically through all the possible choices, starting with an x value and trying out each possible y value until the area becomes too big.

x	y	$2x + 4y - 8$		x	y	$2x + 4y - 8$
5	3	14 ✓		7	3	18 ✓
5	4	18 ✓		7	4	22 ✗
5	5	22 ✗		8	3	20 ✗
6	3	16 ✓				
6	4	20 ✗				

Possible solutions are: $x = 5, y = 3$ $x = 5, y = 4$
$\qquad\qquad\qquad\qquad x = 6, y = 3$ $x = 7, y = 3$

8.2.3 Modelling With Trigonometry

Example 5: Using a Right Angled Triangle   **G**

A vertical flag pole of height 5.8 m is to be supported by a wire rope fastened to the top and to a point on the ground.
The safety regulations state that a support wire should make an angle of between 45° and 55° with the ground.
Would a wire support of length 7.5 m be acceptable?

Solution:

Draw a diagram to help you to see what is required.

Check out the situation using a wire of the size given.
Let $x°$ be the angle the wire of length 7.5 m makes with the ground.

You could also check out what length would be required for angles of 45° and 55°, but this involves more calculations.

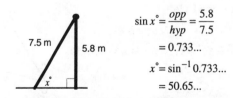

$$\sin x° = \frac{opp}{hyp} = \frac{5.8}{7.5}$$
$$= 0.733...$$
$$x° = \sin^{-1} 0.733...$$
$$= 50.65...$$

This wire would make an angle of 50.7° (to 1 dp) with the ground, which is within the range of acceptable values of 45° to 55°.
Therefore it would make an acceptable support.
Notice the specific reference to the conditions (underlined).

Questions involving the Triangle Rules often use bearings to set up a diagram, possibly also making use of the special angle results (see Section 4.1.4).
The solution will then be obtained by using the Sine Rule or the Cosine Rule.

Example 6: Using the Trig Rules

[C]

A ship sails from port A for 35 km on a bearing of 120°, and then for 54 km on a bearing of 250°. How far is it from the port now?

Solution:

Make a sketch, using the bearings and distances.

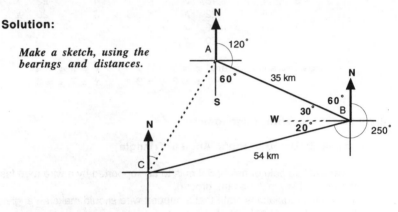

Identify the basic triangle and add information about as many sides and angles as possible.
The additional information has been added in bold to the diagram above, and was obtained as follows:

$$NAB = 120°, \text{ so } SAB = 60°$$
$$ABN = 60° \text{ (alternate angles), so } ABW = 30°$$
$$CB \text{ is on bearing of } 250°, \text{ so } CBW = 20°$$
$$\text{Angle } ABC = 30 + 20 = 50°$$

Use the Cosine Rule in triangle ABC to find AC.

By the Cosine Rule,

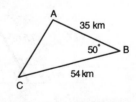

$$b^2 = a^2 + c^2 - 2ac\cos B$$
$$b^2 = 54^2 + 35^2 - 2 \times 54 \times 35 \times \cos 50°$$
$$= 1711.2...$$
$$b = \sqrt{1711.2...}$$
$$= 41.36...$$

Side AC is 41.4 km to 1 dp.

The ship is now **41.4 km** from the port.

8.2.4 Modelling With Geometry

Example 7: Using a Right Angled Triangle

While orienteering, a girl chose to detour around
a marshy area by following 2 bearings at right
angles to each other, as shown.
She ran round the detour at 3.5 m/s and
estimated that she would have run across the
marshy area at 2.5 m/s.
Was her choice a good one? Justify your answer.

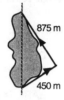

Solution:

Draw a diagram to help you see what is required.
Use Pythagoras to find the length of the 'marsh' route.

By Pythagoras,

$$d^2 = 450^2 + 875^2$$
$$= 968\,125$$
$$d = \sqrt{968\,125}$$
$$= 983.9...$$

Work out the time taken round each route.
Make it clear which is which.

By detour :   Total distance $= 450 + 875 = 1325$ m

Speed $= 3.5$ m/s

$$T = \frac{D}{S} = \frac{1325}{3.5}$$
$$= 378.57...$$

By marsh :   Distance $= 983.9...$ m

Speed $= 2.5$ m/s

$$T = \frac{D}{S} = \frac{983.9...}{2.5}$$
$$= 393.56...$$

It was a good choice because it took her **379 s** by the detour, and it would
have taken **394 s** across the marsh, **15 s** more.

Problem Solving

Example 8: Using Circle Geometry

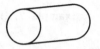

An oil tank is cylindrical in shape with radius 130 cm
and length 500 cm. It sits with the length horizontal.
The tank has an 'oil-low' indicator which buzzes when
there is a depth of 10 cm of oil left.
What volume of oil is left in the tank when the indicator sounds?

Solution:

*Draw a diagram first and name points with letters to
make the working easier to follow.*

$\triangle ABC$ is right angled at B. Let $w = BC$.

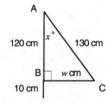

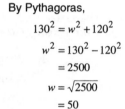

By Pythagoras,

$$130^2 = w^2 + 120^2$$
$$w^2 = 130^2 - 120^2$$
$$= 2500$$
$$w = \sqrt{2500}$$
$$= 50$$

$\angle BAC = x°$

$$\tan x° = \frac{opp}{adj} = \frac{50}{120}$$
$$= 0.416...$$
$$x° = \tan^{-1} 0.416...$$
$$= 22.6...°$$

*You need to find the area of the segment cut off by CD.
The standard method for this is to find the area of sector ADC and
subtract the area of triangle ADC.*

Angle DAC = 2 x 22.6... = 45.2...°

Area of sector ADC

$$= \frac{45.2...}{360} \times \text{area of circle}$$
$$= \frac{45.2...}{360} \times \pi r^2$$
$$= \frac{45.2...}{360} \times \pi \times 130^2$$
$$= 6671.9...$$

Base = $2BC = 100$

Area of $\triangle$ ADC
$$= \tfrac{1}{2} \times \text{base} \times \text{height}$$
$$= \tfrac{1}{2} \times 100 \times 120$$
$$= 6000$$

Cross-section area of oil = area of sector ADC − area of $\triangle$ADC
$$= 6671.9... - 6000$$
$$= 671.9...$$

Volume of oil = area x length
$$= 671.9... \text{ x } 500$$
$$= 335\ 984.9...$$
$$= \textbf{336 litres} \text{ to nearest litre}\ (1000\ cm^3 = 1\ \text{litre})$$

8.3 PROVING A RESULT

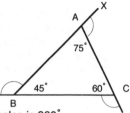

You may be asked to check a result holds for particular values but then to **prove that the result is true for all values**. Proof is a very important concept in maths.

It is **not** enough to check it out for a few more values. You must **generalise,** ie work with symbols and show that it holds. Only then can you say it is true for all values.

Example 9:

Angle XAC is called the **external angle at A.**

Similarly angle YBA is the external angle at B and angle ZCB is the external angle at C.

(a) In the triangle ABC with angles as shown, show that the sum of the 3 external angles is $360°$.

(b) Prove that for any triangle, the sum of the external angles is $360°$.

Solution:

(a)

$$\angle XAC = 180 - 75 = 105°$$
$$\angle YBA = 180 - 45 = 135°$$
$$\angle ZCB = 180 - 60 = 120°$$

Sum of external angles $= 105° + 135° + 120° = 360°$

(b) *Now repeat, using letters, exactly what you have just done with numbers.*

Let $\angle BAC = a°$, $\angle CBA = b°$, $\angle ACB = c°$.

$$\angle XAC = (180 - a)°$$
$$\angle YBA = (180 - b)°$$
$$\angle ZCB = (180 - c)°$$

Sum of external angles $= (180 - a)° + (180 - b)° + (180 - c)°$

$$= 180° + 180° + 180° - a° - b° - c°$$
$$= 540° - (a + b + c)°$$
$$= 540° - 180°$$

(sum of angles in $\triangle = 180°$)

$$= 360°$$

So the sum of the external angles will be $360°$ for any triangle.

See also Section 8.2.2 (Modelling with "Show That ..." Questions).

Problem Solving

8.4 "JUSTIFY..." / "GIVE A REASON ..." / "EXPLAIN..." QUESTIONS

Many R&E questions ask you to **justify your answer**, or **give a reason** for it.
There is a great variety in these types of questions, and only a few can be shown here.
See also Examples 3, 5, 7 and 19.

In each case, you must answer the question, <u>making specific reference</u> to any
conditions given. It is important that both your working and your conclusion make your
thinking clear as to why you have given this answer.

Example 10: Using Percentages

A door-to-door salesman has been given a target of calling at 85% of the houses in
a certain area in 1 week.
There are 970 houses in the area. He estimates that each house visit should take
an average of two and a half minutes. He plans to work a 5 day week starting at
9 am each day and working until 5 pm, with one hour off for lunch.
Will his plan allow him to meet his target? Explain your answer.

Solution:

Hours of work per day = 7   Hours of work per week = 5 x 7 = 35

Minutes of work per week = 35 x 60 = 2100

Number of visits per week = 2100 ÷ 2.5 = 840

Target = 85% of 970 = 0.85 x 970 = 824.5

Yes, his plan will let him make his target, as he will visit 840 houses and his
target was to visit 825 houses.

Example 11: Using a Trig Function

The depth of water, d metres, in a harbour, h hours after noon, is given by the
formula: $d(h) = 2.5 - 2\sin(30h + 40)^\circ$

Could a boat which requires a water level of 3.5 m enter the harbour at 5.30 pm?
Justify your answer.

Solution:

At 5.30 pm , $h = 5.5$ $d(h) = 2.5 - 2\sin(30h + 40)^\circ$

$$d(5.5) = 2.5 - 2\sin(30 \times 5.5 + 40)^\circ$$
$$= 2.5 - 2\sin(205)^\circ$$
$$= 3.34...$$

No, the boat could not enter the harbour at 5.30 pm, as there is only 3.3 m of
water at that time and it requires 3.5 m.

8.5 MAKING COMPARISONS

Questions of this type require a comparison to be made between different possibilities, and a choice to be made as to the 'best'.

It is important that the choice is clearly supported mathematically.

Example 12: Comparing for Best Value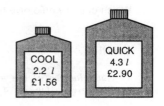

A shop sells 2 brands of orange juice, Cool Juice and Quick Juice, as shown.

(a) Using the information on the labels, explain which <u>appears</u> to give better value for money.

The small print on the labels tells you that the Cool Juice must be mixed 1 part juice to 4 parts water, and Quick Juice is mixed 1 part juice to 3 parts water.

(b) How does this information affect your decision as to which is the better value? You must show all your working.

Solution:

In examples like this, you must find a common method of comparison. The simplest to work with here is cost per litre.
Be careful to divide cost by number of litres to obtain this.

You must also work to enough accuracy to make the comparison - a fraction of a penny. It may help to work in pence rather than pounds.

Your working must indicate clearly which quantity you are working on and what you are doing.

(a) Cool: cost per litre = 156 ÷ 2.2 = 70.9... p per litre of juice
Quick: cost per litre = 290 ÷ 4.3 = 67.4... p per litre of juice

The **Quick Juice** is cheaper per litre, so it **appears to give better value**.

(b) Cool: 1:4 makes 5 times the amount, ie makes 5 x 2.2 = 11 litres of drink
cost per litre = 156 ÷ 11 = 14.1... p per litre of drink
Quick: 1:3 makes 4 times the amount, ie makes 4 x 4.3 = 17.2 litres of drink
cost per litre = 290 ÷ 17.2 = 16.8... p per litre of drink

The **Cool Juice** is cheaper per litre for the actual drink, so it **gives better value**.

Example 13: Comparing Rates of Appreciation

An executive is offered a 3 year contract with 2 salary options:

EITHER   A - a starting salary of £35 000 with an increase of 4.5% at the end of each year,

OR   B - a starting salary of £30 000 with an increase of 15% at the end of each year.

Which option would give her the greater income over the 3 year contract?

Solution:

Note the use of the multiplier 1.045 to give the effect of a 4.5% increase. This gives 100% + 4.5% in one step and saves time (see Section 2.3.3).

You can work out 4.5% separately and add it to the previous salary if you prefer.

OPTION A		OPTION B	
1st year salary	$= £35\,000$	1st year salary	$= £30\,000$
2nd year salary	$= 1.045 \times 35\,000$	2nd year salary	$= 1.15 \times 30\,000$
	$= £36\,575$		$= £34\,500$
3rd year salary	$= 1.045 \times 36\,575$	3rd year salary	$= 1.15 \times 34\,500$
	$= £38\,220.88$		$= £39\,675$
Total salary $=$		Total salary $=$	
	$35\,000 + 36\,575 + 38\,220.88$		$30\,000 + 34\,500 + 39\,675$
	$= £109\,795.88$		$= £104\,175$

Option A gives the greater income over the 3 year contract.

8.6 QUALITATIVE GRAPHING

When you plot graphs point by point, you are graphing information **quantitatively**.

When you use a sketch to show the general shape of a graph, often without making use of scales, you are graphing information **qualitatively**.

Often you will be required to show how one graph compares with another, eg steeper, higher, etc and it is helpful to show both graphs on the same set of axes.

Although the graph may be a sketch, it still needs to be neatly drawn.

Example 14: Plotting Points

The graph shows some information about two players in a football team, Fernando and Cutter. Fernando cost more.

(a) Label the points with the names of the footballers.

(b) What else does the graph tell you about the players?

The club buy a new player, Hacker. He has scored as many goals as Cutter, and cost less than Fernando, but more than Cutter.

(c) Show this information by marking a point on the graph.

Solution:

(a) See graph.
Fernando must be the higher point since he cost more.

(b) **Cutter has scored more goals**.
Cutter is further to the right on the 'goals scored' axis.

(c) See graph.
Hacker must be the same distance to the right as Cutter, since they scored the same number of goals. He should be in between the heights of Cutter and Fernando since his cost is in between the two.

Problem Solving

Example 15: Sketching Graphs

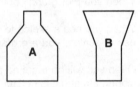

Water is poured into container A at a constant rate. The depth of water in the container is recorded as the water is poured in, and a graph of depth against time is drawn (shown with the solid line in the graph).

(a) Copy the graph of A and on it show how the depth of water in container B would change if it was filled at the same rate.

The dotted line in the graph shows how the depth of water in a third container, C, changed as it was being filled at the same rate.

(b) Sketch the shape of container C.

Solution:

Hints: From the graph of A, note that:

- *while the sides are vertical, the depth changes at a constant rate so the graph gives a straight line,*

- *the narrower the container the steeper the line,*

- *if the width of the bottle is changing, the graph will give a curve.*

(a) The bottle is narrow at the bottom so the graph should start steeper and straight. The bottle then widens, so the graph will then curve to become less steep. See graph.

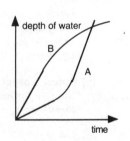

(b) The graph of C is starting steep, but curving, becoming less steep.

The bottle will start narrow but become wider.

The graph then curves to become steeper.

The bottle will then change to become narrower again. See sketch.

8.7 USING PATTERNS

In examples of this type, you must look to see what patterns are present and then use the same patterns to create the required ones.

If a general case involving a letter is requested, then do to the letter exactly what you did to the numbers.

Example 16: Using Patterns

c

The following patterns can be used to sum the consecutive cube whole numbers.

$$1^3 + 2^3 = \frac{2^2 \times 3^2}{4}$$

$$1^3 + 2^3 + 3^3 = \frac{3^2 \times 4^2}{4}$$

$$1^3 + 2^3 + 3^3 + 4^3 = \frac{4^2 \times 5^2}{4}$$

(a) Express $1^3 + 2^3 + 3^3 + ... + 15^3$ in the same way.

(b) The first n cube numbers are added. Find a formula for the total.

Solution:

(a) *Look for any patterns in the given examples:*
  - *always a fraction with 4 in the denominator,*
  - *the first number in the top line is the same as the last cube number,*
  - *the second number on the top line is 1 more than first,*
  - *both top line numbers are squared.*

So $\qquad 1^3 + 2^3 + 3^3 + ... + 15^3 = \dfrac{\mathbf{15^2 \times 16^2}}{\mathbf{4}}$

(b) The first n cube numbers will finish with n^3.

So the first number on the top line will be n.
The next will be $n+1$.

So $\qquad 1^3 + 2^3 + 3^3 + ... + n^3 = \dfrac{\mathbf{n^2 \times (n+1)^2}}{\mathbf{4}}$

8.8 ORGANISED LISTING

Questions which involve checking out a variety of possible answers should be approached in a systematic way to ensure that no answer is missed, or used twice.

Example 17: Organised Listing

G

The SCOTSFARE company are planning to sell a gift box selection of 3 of their specialities. The value of the food in each gift box is to be between £5 and £6 and each box must contain at least one of each of the following:
  Shortbread £2,   Tinned Salmon £1.10,   Scotch Broth Soup 50p.

(a) Complete the table to show all the different ways of making up the gift box.

Shortbread £2.00	Salmon £1.10	Scotch Broth Soup 50p	Total Cost (£)
2	1	1	5.60

(b) The final cost of the selection box is to include postage at 25p per item. Which combination would give the lowest final cost?

Solution:

(a) *Work systematically through all the possibilities. For example, the maximum number of Shortbread is 2. This allows 1 of each of the others. Now reduce the Shortbread to 1. This allows a maximum of 3 Salmon with 1 Soup. Continue like this to find all the possibilities.*

Shortbread £2.00	Salmon £1.10	Scotch Broth Soup 50p	Total Cost (£)	Cost including Postage
2	1	1	5.60	6.60
1	3	1	5.80	7.05
1	2	3	5.70	7.20
1	2	2	5.20	6.45
1	1	5	5.60	7.35
1	1	4	5.10	6.60

(b) *It helps to add a column for Cost including Postage.*

Postage is added at 25p per item, eg the first line has 4 items, so postage costs an extra £1.

From the table, the cheapest overall cost would be **1 shortbread, 2 salmon** and **2 soups** at **£6.45**.

8.9 EXTENDED PROBLEMS

Some questions become R&E questions because of their complexity. They may involve two or three different processes which have to be worked through in order to reach a final answer.

It is important to try and break the problem down into steps, but also to keep an overview of the whole problem. It is very easy in an exam to complete one step and think you have finished the whole problem!

It often helps to work <u>backwards</u> through a problem and think what you would need for each part.

Example 18: Circles and S,D,T

The length of a running track is measured round the <u>inside</u> of the lane.
An athlete ran 4 laps of this circuit in 3 min and 45 s.
Calculate his average speed in m/s.

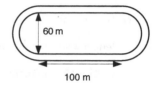

Solution:

To find speed, you need to know distance and time. The time is given. You need to work out the distance run. To find that, you need to know the distance round the track. It is made up from 2 straights and 2 semi-circles. You must first find the circumference of a whole circle equivalent to the 2 semi-circles.

$$d = 60m \qquad C = \pi d \qquad\qquad 3 \text{ min } 45 \text{ s} = 225 \text{ s}$$
$$= \pi \times 60$$
$$= 188.4...$$

Distance round the track = 2 straights + 2 semi − circles
$$= 2 \times 100 + 2 \times 0.5 \times 188.4...$$
$$= 388.4...$$
Distance 4 times round $= 4 \times 388.4...$
$$= 1553.9...$$

$$\text{Average speed} = \frac{\text{distance}}{\text{time}} = \frac{1553.9...}{225}$$
$$= 6.90...$$

His average speed was **6.9 m/s** to 1 dp.

Example 19: 3D Solids and Packing Problems Ⓖ

Cylindrical tin cans of soup with a diameter of 8 cm and a height of 15 cm have to be packed <u>upright</u> in a box.
The box has length 80 cm, width 48 cm and height 30 cm.
A camp requires 100 litres of soup to feed the campers.
Would one box of soup be enough? Explain your answer.

Solution:

You need to know the amount of soup in the box.
To find that you need to know the amount of soup in 1 tin and the number of tins in the box.
To find the number of tins you need to consider how many will pack in each direction.

Number of tins:

length = 80   number of tins along length = $80 \div 8 = 10$

width = 48   number of tins along width = $48 \div 8 = 6$

height = 30   number of tins up height = $30 \div 15 = 2$

So number of tins = $10 \times 6 \times 2 = 120$

Radius of a tin = $8 \div 2 = 4$ cm

Volume of soup in 1 tin $= \pi r^2 h = \pi \times 4^2 \times 15$
$= 753.9...$

Volume of soup in 120 tins $= 120 \times 753.9...$
$= 90\ 477.8...\ \text{cm}^3$
$= 90.47...\ \text{litres}$

No, one box would not be enough as it gives 90.5 litres (to 1 dp), which is less than the 100 litres required.

Example 20: Using Trig and Circle Results

A boy wishes to make a triangle out of a length
of metal to hold the 15 red snooker balls.

Each ball has a diameter of 5.0 cm.

By considering how the corner ball fits into the triangle,
find the length of metal required to make the triangle.

Solution:

*Make a sketch, concentrating on how the ball fits into the corner.
Use the information given and the circle geometry results to identify a right
angled triangle.*

The big triangle is equilateral, so each
angle is 60°.

The line AC bisects the angle, so angle
CAB = 30°.

CB is a radius meeting a tangent, so
angle ABC = 90°.

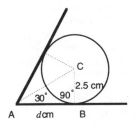

In the right angled triangle ABC,

$$\tan 30° = \frac{opp}{adj} = \frac{2.5}{d}$$

$$d\tan 30° = 2.5$$

$$d = \frac{2.5}{\tan 30°} = 4.33...$$

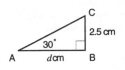

*Be careful considering how the side of the equilateral triangle is made up.
There is a "d" length at each end with a radius of a ball next to it, plus 3
full balls (6 radii). Use the drawing in the question to help you.*

Side length of equilateral triangle $= 2d + 8r$

$$= 2 \times 4.33... + 8 \times 2.5$$

$$= 28.66...$$

Total length of equilateral triangle

$$= 3 \times 28.66...$$

$$= 85.98...$$

Length of metal required is **86 cm** to the nearest cm.

Detailed Index A - Z